# PRAISE FOR *THE JOY IN BUSINESS*

"Joy Baldridge has an infectious enthusiasm blended with a wealth of business experience, and she has delightfully brought the two together in *The Joy in Business*. Some of her wisdom pearls were acquired early in life from her successful businessman-continuous-learner dad, and the rest from a lifetime of observing the human condition in corporate America and beyond. Whether it's learning about the "Purple Break" as a means of reenergizing body and soul or "salting the hay"—a metaphor for creative adaptation—you will find *The Joy in Business* a delightful guide to a better, happier, and more effective tomorrow."

Charles V. Firlotte, president and CEO, Aquarion Water Company

"We saw a $500k ROI in the first two weeks because what Joy teaches actually worked in the field from the very first day. Joy's background as a linguist, combined with her personal success in sales, lends credence to her real-world strategies, which were easily adopted by our team."

Angela Kreps, vice president, strategic business,
Sekisui XenoTech, LLC

"If you want great advice that you can actually apply to your own life to make it even better, *The Joy in Business* is a *must-read*. I loved reading this book! This is not just an ordinary book that regurgitates what you've heard in the past; this book offers great actionable tips that you can apply immediately to your own life to make it even better! I especially liked the Purple Break. I'm using that! I also really like how the book sounds. The way it's written makes it sound like Joy is talking to me personally."

Nick "Sunshine" Tokman, seen on *Deadliest Catch*,
and celebrity keynote speaker

"For me, Joy's delightful book, *The Joy in Business*, is like a bowl of bites of positivity. Using her "Flip and Point" method, you don't have to eat the whole bowl at once; just take a bite when you feel the need. The ideas and tips in this book are quick and effective attitude boosters. Joy does it again!"

Joe Calloway, author, *The Leadership Mindset*

"I have known Joy for several years. I hired her to coach and train our management team. Joy's advice is spot on. She not only motivated my group but led them down a path we had never been on. We like what she did so much we worked with her to develop a whole new management training program completely customized for our group. The results where staggering. She moved the needle. We got our managers to another level. I couldn't have been more pleased. Joy is an outstanding and true person. She comes from a place where other speakers/authors don't and helps all immeasurably with her innovative tools."

Kent Hanley, CEO, Coldwell Banker Howard Perry and Walston

"We engaged Joy Baldrige at The Bermuda Tourism Authority's very first team strategy meeting. As a "start-up" we wanted to establish a culture that was positive, entrepreneurial, collaborative, and flexible. Her half-day session helped our team to understand their varied communication and work styles as well as cement a standard of tolerance, versatility, and cooperation. Her energy is exciting, and her method of delivery is designed to reach every level of an organization. Some of the concepts that Joy introduced to our team during that session are still being used today as keystones in our organization. In Joy's book you will experience firsthand what we did in our meeting, and you will achieve powerful results!"

Willa Douglas, human resource manager,
Bermuda Tourism Authority

"If you apply all of Joy's messages during your working day, you will be very successful and happy."

Chris Bailey, PwC director of people and organization,
president of the CISHRP

"This is a book to keep close by and read repeatedly. Each chapter empowers me to have a positive outlook in my everyday interactions —whether it's at work in the hospital, in a business meeting, or communicating with friends and family. Chapter 27 was especially helpful when it comes to putting things in perspective and has kept me from overreacting over and over again. AFA!!! (Chapter 2)."

Mary Schweikert, RN, BSN|Research Nurse Auditor,
HonorHealth Research Institute

"*The Joy in Business* is packed with valuable and easy-to-implement strategies from Joy Baldridge, one of the most respected trainers and speakers in the field. Written with good humor in an easy-to-read format, it combines gems of practical advice with a load of positivity. This is a unique management book that you will be referring to again and again."

Inga Masjule, co-founder, HR Revolution Inc., and former global
executive HR director, Walkers

"I use the Plus, Plus, Dash and so many of Joy's techniques daily. She creates the most useful and lasting tools to succeed in business and life. Her wisdom lasts a lifetime!"

Kelly Givas, director of Media Relations, Davis Gonthier, Inc.,
formerly of *Architectural Digest*

"Joy Baldridge's techniques and strategies are invaluable across all industries. As someone who works in network television, my day moves rapidly and is ever changing at a moment's notice. Joy's concept of flexibility and adaptability is a vital skill to have to maintain relationships and keep the ship moving at full speed. This book speaks to those just graduating college, as well as those at the top of their careers. After reading this book it is not something you are going to want to put on the shelf. It is a tool that can be kept within arm's reach in your office to save time and increase profit/productivity daily. You can instantly implement the language Joy shares with your employees or co-workers to work better and *happier*. If you live the words and techniques in *The Joy in Business,* I have no doubt that you will find even more success in your work and life. Joy is truly a powerhouse business expert."

Will Hart, Unscripted Series and Specials, TNT/tbs,
Turner Broadcasting System, Inc.

"Joy was wonderful on the TEDx she did for us at UCCI. Her scores were off the charts. The audience absolutely loved her. (But of course!) In her book, *The Joy in Business* she shares her awesome advice and her vibrant personality with the reader, who will benefit greatly."

JD Mosley-Matchett, Ph.D. UCCI

"*The Joy in Business* helps you assess your career energy. It provides useful ways to get rid of negativity and energize yourself. It helps you figure out where you are falling short and how to do the new things at work to make you happier and more productive."

Joann Flynn, MS, CNS, CNC, associate director of sales enablement, IQVIA

"This book is out of this world fantastic! I love it! It pumped me up, made me smile, gave me energy and blew me away!"

Daryl Gross, teacher at The Meadows School, Las Vegas

"As a writer on the late-night talk show *The Arsenio Hall Show*, I was required to write twenty-five jokes each day before noon. Each of Arsenio's other eleven writers on the staff did the same. The best of the jokes made up that night's opening monologue. The monologue was a conglomeration of fine-tuned comedic takes on weekly news topics that together formed a 12-minute entertaining and informed look at the world that week. Likewise, *The Joy in Business* is comprised of informative knowledge nuggets presented in a humorous way … the difference being that *The Joy in Business* can be passed down to your kids as a potential life-changing vehicle, whereas my old *Arsenio Hall Show* scripts are good for only one thing … as a fun excuse for my kids to play with my shredder. *The Joy in Business* provides inspirational victories for us that will help us along the road of life. The overall result is a life-changing experience for the reader."

Art Sears, president, The Art Sears Company/Radio Guest Quest

"It is always so wonderful to reflect on your teachings and to remember the impact they have! These concepts apply to life's situations in many cases and not just to business. The points that you suggest can help you manage the challenging people and situations in the selling of yourself and your ideas in the world. They can provide a better feeling about how one handles work and life. I am a much better person when I used these ideas daily!"

Cindy Rewerts, MS, director of the CMO, Roivant Pharma for Roivant Sciences

"Joy Baldridge is one of the most incredible people I have ever met. Joy is the perfect person to have written *The Joy in Business* because whatever she does in life, be it business, family, having fun with friends, she does it with great, deep, sincere, genuine joy."

Mark Riesenberg, owner/founder, Human Resources Unlimited

"Joy Baldridge is something else! She is funny and smart. Joy was the opening keynote speaker for our convention. Her message resonated with all who attended. This book will make a significant difference in the lives of all who read it."

Gayla Guignard, chief strategy officer, The Alexander Graham Bell Association for the Deaf and Hard of Hearing

"When I was seeking an outside keynote speaker, Joy immediately responded to my online submission requesting a speaker on the topics of Time Management and Effective Communication Skills. Joy called me personally to learn more about the Society of Financial Examiners. She had some actionable techniques that she tailored in her presentations based on the audience members' background. What a pleasure it was to have Joy as our guest speaker at our Career Development Seminar. The information you will discover within the pages of *The Joy in Business* will significantly impact your work and life."

Colette Hogan Sawyer, CFE, CPM, MSA, MCM, co-chair, CDS Program Committee, The Society of Financial Examiners (SOFE)

"What a fabulous resource for business professionals, entrepreneurs, and just about anybody, everywhere! A must read! What a terrific compilation of unique and inspirational ideas to help grow your business and live a more positive, productive, and profitable life! All of Joy's advice, tools, and techniques are very creative and easy to implement. I have had the pleasure of working with Joy professionally and personally for many years, and I know first-hand that she completely opens her arsenal of treasures that has grown her own very successful global speaker/consulting business. Joy is the real deal. Her joyful, energetic spirit exudes on the pages with her golden nuggets of inspiration! *The Joy in Business: Innovative Ideas to Find Positivity (and Profit) in Your Daily Work Life* is sure to remain an inspirational tool on your desk for years to come!."

Lisa Lelas, bestselling author of *Simple Steps: 10 Weeks to Getting Better Control of Your Life* and the Simple Steps book series, speaker/productivity consultant and founder of Bestseller Bootcamp

# The Joy in Business

## Innovative Ideas to Find Positivity (and Profit) in Your Daily Work Life

Joy Baldridge

WILEY

Cover design: Paul McCarthy

For general information on our other products and services or for technical support, please contact our Customer Care Department within the United States at (800) 762-2974, outside the United States at (317) 572-3993 or fax (317) 572-4002.

Wiley publishes in a variety of print and electronic formats and by print-on-demand. Some material included with standard print versions of this book may not be included in e-books or in print-on-demand. If this book refers to media such as a CD or DVD that is not included in the version you purchased, you may download this material at http://booksupport.wiley.com. For more information about Wiley products, visit www.wiley.com.

*Library of Congress Cataloging-in-Publication Data has been applied for and is on file with the Library of Congress.*
ISBN 9781119528579 (Hardcover)
ISBN 9781119528562 (ePDF)
ISBN 9781119528555 (ePub)

Printed in the United States of America
V10005956_110918

*This book is dedicated with love to Bill, Wilson, Mackenzie, Jonas, Kelly, Haley, Will, Jesse, Lucky, and Winter McAlarney, Lila and Ken Baldridge, and YOU, for continuing to bring more joy to the business world by being in it and positively contributing to it.*

# DON'T READ THIS BOOK

N o time to read while on the go?

Why read, when you can Flip and Point?

## THE FLIP AND POINT

The Flip and Point is an innovative way to get quick tips fast. It randomly provides you with useful ideas that you were meant to receive because it is a universe connection versus a deliberate act.

I discovered the value of the Flip and Point when I was preparing for a presentation and, with seconds to spare, I flipped and pointed to a section of a reference book. Voila, I found a very useful idea that I still use today. Why pressure yourself to read a whole book when you can find quick, tangible tools you can immediately use by flipping and pointing?

Give it a try now. Flip the pages of this book. (You can close your eyes while doing this if you wish.) Point to a word on a page, then read the paragraph. See if it speaks to you. If so, great! If not, flip and point again. Three flip and points is a good amount to do to get some fresh ideas.

Of course, you can also read this book the traditional way, one page at a time. It is designed to be reader-friendly with brief chapters and inspirational quotes. Please let me know your favorite "Golden Nuggets" that you discover along the way via email: joy@joybaldridge.com.

# WARNING!

This book comes with a warning. My parents raised me to be a positive, optimistic person, but my dad said, "Being positive and optimistic comes with a warning." I said, "What's the warning?" He said, "If you are too happy all the time, people can't take it! They'll just want to slap you."

"Really!?" I asked.

He said, "They will think you are delusional, hard to relate to, or drinking. Be positive, but in degrees, not over the top." Apply the useful ideas you read in these pages. They are designed to help you lead a more happy and productive life. Enjoy the joy it brings you. But in degrees, not overly so.

# QUICK TOOLS GUIDE

- To reduce anxiety and stress turn to Chapter 4 and get rid of your WAFs.
- To get quick advice from musician John Mayer turn to Chapter 17.
- To be a better listener take the listening quiz in Chapter 17.
- To deal with difficult people turn to Chapter 14 and learn that people are different more than difficult.
- To increase sales turn to Chapter 14 and learn about Velvet Hammer words and Chapter 21 to learn exceptional ways to present.
- To save time turn to Chapter 18 and discover the plus, plus, dash.
- To be a better leader, business professional, or person, read the book in its entirety and keep it nearby for quick reference and advice. You'll be glad you did!

# CONTENTS

# CONTENTS

# PREFACE

The purpose of this book is to provide you with an abundance of life-changing fresh ideas; inspirational, thought-provoking, humorous stories; and quotes in an instant. Each chapter is designed to be read and absorbed quickly. You will discover problem-solving solutions and specific actions to take to find positivity (and profit) in your daily work and life.

Regardless of how long you have been in the working world or the line of work or industry you are in, whether it is management, sales, finance, science, research, manufacturing, healthcare, retail, publishing, technology, customer service, hospitality, startup or entrepreneurial ventures, the ideas, stories, and quotes can be successfully applied to create a more positive and successful way of working and living.

## DIRECT APPLICATION

The techniques and strategies within these pages can be used as a coping mechanism when faced with adversity, as a motivational tool to forge ahead, as a focal point to keep perspective, and as the foundation to building a positive culture of clear and respectful communication, integrity, and sustainable change in any organization.

## INSTANT PERSPECTIVE AND
## BEHAVIOR CHANGE

You can have an instant perspective and behavior change by reading this book and selecting and applying the Golden Nuggets, precious simple Joy Gems, that can transform your thoughts, actions, and life in an instant. Doing this will build momentum toward furthering your success for tomorrow. The key is to be flexible and adaptable.

AFA all the way! Always Flexible and Adaptable.
HAPPY READING!

JOY Baldridge, CPC, CSP

# GRATITUDE

There are so many people to whom I am eternally grateful for helping bring this book to fruition. The encouragement of Will Hart, Louise McQuillan, and Eileen Arndt at the office. Lila and Ken Baldridge, Joe Calloway, and Matt Holt at John Wiley & Sons, who quickly made the right connections at Wiley. To Jeanenne Ray for getting contract approval in record time, and for her positive attitude and marketing wisdom. To Vicki Adang for her editing expertise, project management skills, and being so positive and fun to work with. To Danielle Serpica for keeping things running swiftly and smoothly. To Peter Knox for his marketing expertise. To Dawn Kilgore for expert production and content prowess, ensuring each stage of production went smoothly and on schedule, and to Rebecca Taff for swiftly expediting the prepress set-up process. To Christie Fountain for proofing. To Mary Schweikert, Sue Hasham, Mark Riesenberg, Holly Grounds, Wendy Hughes, Joann Flynn, Art and Maribeth Sears, Sue Cronin, Mary, Shiela, and Sharon Sullivan, Kendra Feshbach, Inga Masjule, Chris Bailey, Daryl Gross, Simone Morris, Lesslie Burhans, Mary Saunders, Donna Bush, Donna Mitchell, Janette Goodman, Tabitha Philander, and Nina Moscow for treasured friendships.

# PART 1

# 1

# THE PURPLE BREAK

 **Q.** Are you ever tired? Ever wake up tired? Have that mid-afternoon lull? Go to bed tired?

**A.** You probably need a Purple Break.

What's a Purple Break? A Purple Break is a unique technique that my father, Ken Baldridge, developed to restore energy and ignite action.

Dad was in a sleep study in the 1960s where he was instructed to sleep in a room in total darkness for three months. During the day, he could work as he usually did, but as part of the study, thick black drapes were put on the windows of his bedroom so he could sleep in total darkness.

He noticed, gradually, over time, that he was feeling more energetic and less fatigued. He wondered why. He learned that there is a protein in your eyes called rhodopsin, also called visual purple, known to break down in bright light, which causes fatigue. It is restored by total darkness. (For more information about rhodopsin and fatigue on the job, see the Appendix.)

After the study was complete, he found he only needed to sleep three to five hours a night and felt terrific! But as he began traveling to colleges to speak and meet with his clients (he was the founder of the Baldridge Reading and Study Strategy programs) he noticed that he needed more and more sleep. As a dynamic educator and driven entrepreneur, this was frustrating to him.

He realized that the reason he required more sleep was because he was sleeping in hotels where the exterior light could stream through curtains that were thin. Also, there were other light sources in the room that interfered with the restoration of his visual purple, such as a glowing alarm clock, fire alarm light, etc. So he decided to wear an eye shield at night to block out the light, and during the day create a totally dark environment by covering his eyes, four to six times a day, for a few minutes each time, to restore the visual purple.

By doing this he felt more energetic.

He originally called this rest break "visual purple restoration" and taught it to college freshmen to help them study better, especially when cramming before exams. But the name was too long to remember, so he shortened it to Purple Break.

For the last 40 years of his life, my dad required only three to five hours of sleep and had lots of energy.

Give it a try to see how it can work for you.

Grab your phone. Set the alarm for 60 seconds. Now cover your eyes, relax, and breathe. Count backward from 15 to 1 on each breath. For example: Say 15, then exhale, say 14 and exhale. Remember to relax your shoulders and jaw, as they are tension holders. Also, when you reach the number 1, keep your eyes closed and slowly remove your hands. See whether you notice an intense brightness from removing your hands. That brightness is diminishing your rhodopsin.

Ready for your Purple Break experience? Great! Then put this book down, start your timer, and enjoy!

How do you feel? Did you notice the brightness when you were finished and removed your hands from your eyes?

The bright lights in your day, such as sunlight, glowing computer screens, and fluorescent lights wear you down all day long.

One challenge with the Purple Break is that it is not socially acceptable to have your head in your hands. The body language could cause some to think you are upset. If you choose to use this precious Joy Gem, it is best to do it in a discrete place such as a rest room or empty conference room, or office. It is the first Joy Gem in this book because it will refresh you to absorb the other "Golden Nuggets" better.

I once was driving and was so tired I couldn't remember how long it had been since my last blink, which scared me. Has that ever happened to you? So I pulled over on the side of the parkway in a safe area to take a Purple Break. Head in hands, a few minutes later a knock on the window of my car startled me. I looked up and it was a police officer. I opened the window. He said, "Is everything OK?"

I said, "Yes, officer. I'm just taking a Purple Break."

He looked at me suspiciously and said, "And I have a line for you to walk."

Oh no! I thought. So I asked him, "Are you ever tired, Officer?"

He answered, "Yes. I'm tired now."

I went on to ask, "Did you know you have a protein in your eye called rhodopsin that breaks down in bright light and is restored in total darkness?" He did not. Net/net: I didn't have to walk the line. Moral of the story. Be careful where you take your Purple Breaks, but be sure to take them. They are life savers in so many ways.

## Take Action!

1. Figure out where, when, and how you can take Purple Breaks in your day.

2. Look for light sources where you sleep. Minimize/Eliminate.

3. Get an eye shield and wear it.

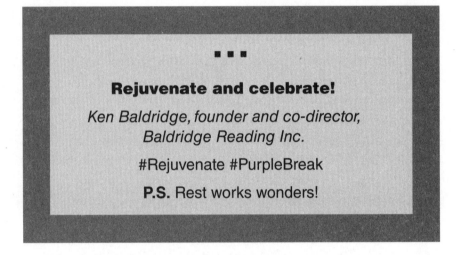

**. . .**

### Rejuvenate and celebrate!

*Ken Baldridge, founder and co-director, Baldridge Reading Inc.*

#Rejuvenate #PurpleBreak

**P.S.** Rest works wonders!

# 2

# AFA ALL
# THE WAY!

**Q.** Do you ever feel stressed out? Burnt out? Sick? I saw a bumper sticker that said, "Ran out of sick days, so tomorrow I'm calling in dead." Another one said, "I feel so much better now that I've given up hope." You can't do that! What can you do?

**A.** You can be flexible and adaptable.

# Always Flexible
# and Adaptable

AFA All the Way! According to *Fortune* magazine, you need to possess two characteristics in order to be successful in this millennium—flexibility and adaptability. If you're rigid, you break, your relationships break, and what good is it to be broken?

Now more than ever, it is key to be flexible and adaptable, like BOB. His name is BOB, but he spells it backwards. (A little palindrome humor.) BOB is the little yellow stretchy stress guy that audience members receive wherever I speak (see Figure 2.1). When pulled, he can stretch far. What's more important is how quickly he bounces back from being stretched to the max. Because he is rubbery he can snap back as fast as a rubber band does. How fast can you bounce back from adversity?

**Flexibility** means to bend without breaking.

**Adaptability** means to adjust to circumstance.

At Baldridge Seminars International, a learning and development organization I founded, we test and embody all the ideas we share with tens of thousands of people at events, conferences, and corporate meetings where I speak throughout the world. I tell the participants, "Flexibility and adaptability are essential to your well-being and success in work and life."

So when you are stuck in traffic and running late, once you check in, it helps to tell yourself, "It's OK, because I am flexible and adaptable."

**Figure 2.1    BOB sticks around (on the young woman's forehead).**

If you're on a tight deadline and the pressure is mounting, try saying to yourself, "It's OK, because I'm flexible and adaptable!" Notice how it feels. Of course some things are not OK, but the point is that *you're* OK. When you handle adversity from a point of calm rationality, it makes for better outcomes.

When we decided to make flexibility and adaptability a cornerstone practice of our organization, we wanted a catchy acronym to make it memorable, so we came up with "AFA All the Way! Always Flexible and Adaptable." I questioned the notion of "always." It seemed unrealistic. This concept was unintentionally put to a test when I was scheduled to meet on a Saturday with one of my colleagues, Will Hart, who helped me coin the phrase AFA. He had to pull a lot of strings to be available that day.

An hour before we were going to meet, my daughter had an asthma attack and had to be taken to the doctor right away. She recovered quickly, but I felt terrible canceling the meeting after the extra effort my colleague had made to attend. I sent a text apologizing profusely for inconveniencing him. I knew he would understand, but I still felt bad. (You know that feeling when things don't go as planned and you feel as though you've inconvenienced someone? It can be draining.) His text reply consisted of just three letters: "AFA."

How did that make me feel? (How would that make *you* feel?) Relieved, happy, and worry-free? Once you embody the AFA philosophy, positive change happens. After seminars that I've conducted, clients adopt the AFA culture code and use it in the subject of emails when running late or needing to reschedule. Some say, "How can you always be flexible and adaptable?" We say, "How can you not?"

---

### Take Action!

1. Next time you feel like things are not going as planned, tell yourself, "It's OK because I am flexible and adaptable!"

2. Tell others you know about the AFA code. When changes to your plans occur, text/email/say, "AFA" to validate that you can go with the flow.

3. Become aware that nothing needs to bother you again if you adopt the AFA code of conduct.

---

■ ■ ■

**AFA All the Way. Always be flexible and adaptable, like BOB.**

*Joy Baldridge — Keynote Speaker, TEDx Speaker, and American Author*

#NothingBothersMe

**P.S.** Situations may not be OK, but you're OK!

## Meet BOB

**Q.** How do you bounce back fast from adversity?

**A.** With lightning speed, if you can be like BOB

His name is BOB, but he spells it backwards because he's flexible and adaptable! BOB is a small stretchy yellow stress guy I give out to everyone when I speak (see Figure B.1). Whether there are 10 people in a training class or 10,000 attending a mega conference, everyone receives a BOB. BOB is a reminder and mascot of the AFA philosophy "AFA All the Way! Always Flexible and Adaptable." When I read the *Fortune* magazine article (mentioned in Chapter 2) saying that you need two characteristics to be employed in this millennium, *flexibility* and *adaptability*, it struck me that this was the foundation to great success concept.

Around the same time, I happened to be looking online and saw an adorable little yellow guy and impulsively ordered 200 dozen of them because I thought it would be a great addition to my brand. When the boxes arrived, and I opened one, it was not what I expected. It was sticky and stretchy and there was no face.

**Figure B.1    BOB is the epitome of AFA All the Way!**

Online it had a face that smiled etched in black. These had an embossed face that you couldn't see.

My seven-year-old son Wilson happened to be in the kitchen and, noticing my disappointment, said, "What's wrong, mom?"

I answered, "Well, I bought a lot of these little yellow guys, but it has no face like it did online, and it is sticky, which makes it feel weird."

Wilson picked one up and said, "It has a face; it's just not easy to see."

I said, "You're right. That's because it's embossed."

He pulled the arms and said, "Look, it's really stretchy."

I asked, "Can I give this to an adult business audience?" I always tend to ask my young children business questions to see what they would say. More often than not, they have really good and useful answers, and I take their advice.

He pulled the arms way out and said with a wide grin, "Hey mom, aren't your clients *stretched* for time? Get it, mom? Get it?"

I said, "That's so funny! Yes, I get it." So BOB stays! The next day I took him to the Magazine Publishers of America where some of the most sophisticated editors and advertising sales executive go to learn success strategies.

The first person who came in sat down, picked up BOB, and said, "What is this? It's so sticky." She made a disapproving face and added, "And there's dirt on it." I was mortified. (I learned that because BOB is sticky you have to be careful storing him because he will get dust and dirt attached to him easily.) Luckily, more people entered the conference room and started playing with BOB and liked him (see Figure B.2). So I decided he was going to stay because he is the epitome of flexibility and adaptability.

When you stretch his arms out and let go, he snaps back in an instant, like a rubber band. I use him as an example by asking the audience. "How fast do you bounce back from adversity when you're stretched to the limit? Watch how fast BOB does it." I pull his arms as far as they can go and when I let go, he snaps back fast.

**Figure B.2    People love BOB!**

Ask yourself: "How fast do you snap back from adversity?" and "Can I be more like BOB?"

BOB didn't always have a name. At first, he was referred to as "the little yellow guy" until a fateful day when I was speaking at a manufacturing plant in Dover, Delaware. One of the engineers came into the training room and introduced himself. He said in a serious tone, "Hi, my name is BOB ... but I spell it backwards." I laughed. After that, BOB was born. To take it a step further, his last name is Palindrome. BOB Palindrome.

Although some people don't know that a palindrome is a word that you spell backwards and forwards, I quickly realized that if you have to explain it, it's not as funny. That's probably as much as you need to know about BOB except that he has taken on a life of his own (see Figure B.3).

**Figure B.3    A family of BOBs.**

## BOB Stories

One BOB recipient emailed me that he had a BOB emergency. He had put BOB in his pocket at work and BOB accidently ended up in the washing machine that night and didn't make it successfully through the spin cycle. He had grown attached to BOB and was upset. I told him not to worry, imposed a free BOB replacement plan, and mailed him a fresh new BOB.

A client told me her 10-year old son was having a tough time because of a very difficult and highly contentious divorce that she and her husband were going through. She said, "I have to thank you for BOB. If he didn't have BOB, I don't know how he would make it through. He has been telling me he is going to be flexible and adaptable like BOB." Her son was also being bullied at school during this tough time. He would say, "BOB is my friend. I'll be fine, mom." Her story brought tears to my eyes.

Another mother who attended a seminar later emailed that her daughter was autistic, which made air travel practically impossible. The last time she tried it, she was escorted off the plane because her daughter was acting out so much. The client said she had a family crisis and had no choice but to fly and bring her child. She later told me that she brought the BOB I had given her at the seminar with her and BOB saved the day! All went well. He was the perfect diversion.

School guidance counselors and psychologists have reported they leave BOBs on their desks and the children play with him; it's easier for them to speak openly about what they are dealing with. BOB can be very therapeutic!

BOB is great for team building. When he is brought back to work he is known for sticking to the ceiling, doing yoga, and hanging around as a handy stress toy. Every so often I receive an email that starts with, "You won't believe what happened to BOB . . . ." He's becoming "a thing" (see Figure B.4).

**Figure B.4    Franz Manderson serves as deputy governor of the Cayman Islands and is the Honourable Deputy Governor and Head of the Civil Service.**

# 3

# SALT THE HAY, FIND A WAY!

**Q.** Have you ever felt stuck? Ever have a hard time getting something accomplished or solving a problem?

**A.** You may just need to add a dash of salt. . .

Salt the hay and find a way is a Baldridge family motto.

My father used to use an expression you have probably heard before: You can bring a horse to water, but you can't…. What? Make him drink. Dad would say, "You know what you *can* do?" and I would say, "There is no 'can do' to that."

He would say, "You can salt the hay…. What happens when you salt the hay? If you salt the hay, the horse will get thirsty and drink." Salting the hay is finding a way. There's always a way.

He would say, "Behind every two can'ts there's a can. It's just that most people never find it because the first can't stops them and they say, 'I tried.' And if they make it through that, the second can't stops them because they say, 'I tried again.' What is better is to say, 'If I can't do this, and I can't do that, then what *can* I do?'" This formula unblocks the thought process.

If you remember that behind every two can'ts is a can, you will discover that there usually is one. While working in the Cayman Islands, I was excited to hear the Honourable Deputy Governor and Head of the Civil Service, Franz Manderson (pictured with BOB and me in chapter 2) after attending one of my seminars say that he "salts the hay" in his government cabinet meetings. Upon hearing this, I sent him a large salt shaker to take with him to help emphasize that point!

---

### Take Action!

1. When you find yourself stuck on a situation that you see no way out of, ask yourself, "What can I do?"
2. Remember: Behind every two can't there is a can.
3. There is no try (Yoda). Keep searching for the "can-do."

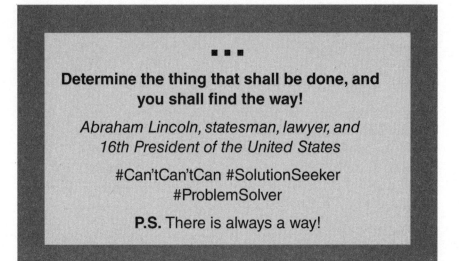

**Determine the thing that shall be done, and you shall find the way!**

*Abraham Lincoln, statesman, lawyer, and 16th President of the United States*

#Can'tCan'tCan #SolutionSeeker #ProblemSolver

**P.S.** There is always a way!

4

# SAY GOODBYE TO YOUR WAFs

**Q.** What would it be like if you never had another worry in the world? What if worry, anxiety, and fear were gone from your life? Would you miss them?

**A.** Maybe yes. Maybe no. To get to no, read below.

# Worry, Anxiety, and Fear

Good-bye, worry, anxiety, and fear.

WAF is an acronym for worry, anxiety, and fear. All three are counter-productive and can make you feel awful! They can also severely and adversely affect your health and physical and psychological well-being unless you decide to rid yourself of them.

According to *Psychology Today*, "90% of what you worry about never even happens." One definition of anxiety is: *the horrible stories we tell ourselves that are rarely if ever true.*

My favorite quote about fear comes from Zig Ziglar, who said that F.E.A.R. can stand for one of two things. **F**ear **E**verything **A**nd **R**un or **F**ace **E**verything **A**nd **R**ise!

Susan Jeffers wrote a book titled *Feel the Fear and Do It Anyway!* I never read the book. I got so much out of that title I didn't have to! I had the book propped up in the office, and every time I walked by it I would say to myself, "Feeling the fear, doing it anyway!"

Defining worry, anxiety, and fear makes it easier to deal with them and cope.

**W**orry is tormenting oneself with disturbing thoughts, usually about real or imagined issues.

**A**nxiety is an emotion characterized by an inner state of emotional turmoil. It is the unpleasant feeling of dreading anticipated events.

**F**ear is a distressing emotion aroused by an immediate threat or impending danger, either real or imagined.

Once you become aware of the degree to which your WAFs affect your work and life, it is vital to determine whether your WAFs are a short-term state or long-term trait.

*States* are temporary behaviors that depend on situations and motives at a certain time.

*Traits* are characteristics, behaviors, and feelings that are consistent and long-lasting.

With awareness, patience, practice, and persistence, you can diminish impulsive states and build positive traits.

Your WAFs are better if they are states, which are fleeting, as opposed to traits that become a part of your character and stay with you indefinitely. Saying "goodbye" to your WAFs helps.

How can you say goodbye to your WAFs? One way is to acknowledge to release. Raise and wave your hand and say, "Goodbye, worry; goodbye, anxiety; so long, fear; and hello, joy!" Can it possibly be as easy as that? Well, yes, it can.

When you acknowledge your WAFs it gives you the power to release them. If you ignore them, they grow and fester. Think of anything that you ignore. Does it ever really go away and get better, or does it stay and build? Ever ignore your laundry? Dishes? Yard? Garden? Bills, taxes, spouse, children, parents, siblings? Co-workers, annoying neighbor, friend? Ever say to yourself, "I'm not going to worry about this!" And then what do you do? Worry about it?

Your worries, anxieties, and fears can make you feel awful! They can drastically affect your physical and psychological well-being unless you decide to rid yourself of them right now. How? See Chapter 5 on PAR.

---

### Take Action!

1. Acknowledge your worry, anxiety, and fear. "I know I am feeling the fear, but I'm OK."

2. Stop. Take a moment and regroup.

3. Ask yourself: "What's the likelihood that this will happen?" More often than not, it won't.

■ ■ ■

**When nothing is certain, anything is possible!**

*Mandy Hale, author and Twitter thought leader and influencer*

**The cave you fear to enter holds the treasure you seek.**

*Joseph Campbell, American professor of literature. Worked in comparative mythology*

■ ■ ■

**Just when you think you know exactly how it's going, some unexpected possibility shows up and it begins to get even better.**

*Andre Pough Sr., author of inspirational books on health and wealth*

#PeaceOfMind

**P.S.** Proclaim yourself WAF-free right now.

**P.P.S.** Cut the worry wires.

5

# PREVENT, ACKNOWLEDGE, AND RELEASE (PAR)

**Q.** Are you on PAR?

**A.** Yes, if you prevent, acknowledge, and release negativity.

Another concept comes into play when dealing with WAFs (worry, anxiety, and fear) — PAR, which stands for prevent, acknowledge, and release. This means *prevent* what you can by thinking ahead, avoiding procrastination, doing your best, being proactive, and empowered.

When things don't go exactly as anticipated, *acknowledge* how you feel by saying, "This stinks. This is so frustrating. This is ridiculous!" Once you acknowledge your feelings, instead of ignoring them, an automatic *release* happens. The auto-release occurs because you are facing your fears instead of trying to dash them. When you face fears, negative thoughts, or circumstances head-on, you will find they don't have as much strength as you thought they did.

You can use PAR in another sense, too: Are you up to PAR? Are you under PAR? PAR is a self-checking device, a standard for performing.

PAR can be a performance and accountability report you do on yourself. It keeps you in check.

---

### Take Action!

1. Acknowledge your WAFs to release them.

2. Relax and breathe!

3. Practice PAR: Prevent–Acknowledge–Release

---

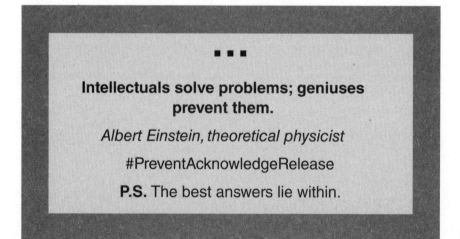

■ ■ ■

**Intellectuals solve problems; geniuses prevent them.**

*Albert Einstein, theoretical physicist*

#PreventAcknowledgeRelease

**P.S.** The best answers lie within.

# 6

# Now Is Perfect

**Q.** Have you ever felt depressed? Of course, you have. Who hasn't?

**A.** The critical time for positive change is now!

# THE CRITICAL TIME IS NOW!

Several years ago, I found myself terribly depressed about everything. Work, marriage, parenting, and basically life in general. A cloud of sadness consumed me that I just couldn't shake. Has that ever happened to you? It was an exhausting and dreadful experience that seemed never-ending. I didn't want to take medication or see anyone about it. I thought that would make it worse.

A friend suggested I contact Stuart, a spiritual guru in Sedona, Arizona. I was so riddled with anxiety that I took the advice and gave Stuart a call. One of the first things Stuart asked was, "What color is your anxiety?" I immediately thought, "Oh no! What have I got myself into?" It seemed like such an obscure question, and I immediately thought it ridiculous and that he potentially was a quack until I blurted out "It's red." Who knew my anxiety had a color? It was a flaming, fiery, scorching hot red.

Stuart said, "Take a breath … and another. Now what color is it?"

I wondered, "Why am I wasting my time with this man? He is way too 'out there' for me." That is, until I replied, "Now it's orange." Realizing that my anxiety really did have a color and that, by breathing, it changed, was interesting.

Stuart said, "Take a breath, and another. There is plenty of air!" I did as he advised. I took a breath and another. He then asked, "What color is it now?"

"Yellow" I replied, amused and bewildered.

"Take a breath and another" he said. I complied.

After about 10 minutes of this process of gentle and focused guided breathing, he asked, "What color is it now?"

I was astonished by my answer. "Gray, like ashes," I replied.

"How do you feel?" he asked.

"Terrific!" I replied. It was a fascinating experience.

He ended our call by saying: "Now is perfect." When I asked what he meant by that, he said that deep breathing puts you in the present tense. It puts you in the "now." Most of the time we use shallow breathing, which causes us to focus on the past or think about the future, so we rarely are truly present.

Now is perfect. Test it any time!

---

### Take Action!

1. Take a breath, take a moment.

2. Be here.

3. Breathe.

---

■ ■ ■

### Now Is Perfect!

*Robert Adams, author and American Advaita teacher*

#BeHereAndBreathe

**P.S.** The critical time is now!

# 7

# 4-4-6
# BREATHING

**Q.** Ever feel overwhelmed? Too much to do? Too little time?

**A.** You need to take a 4–4–6.

The 4–4–6 is a breathing technique that puts you in the present tense. It stops your mind from focusing on any past regrets or angst and prevents you from getting ahead of yourself by slowing down any racing, stressful thoughts about the future.

The 4–4–6 puts you in the "now." Give it a try. Here's how: Inhale. 1, 2, 3, 4. Hold it. 1, 2, 3, 4. Exhale. 1, 2, 3, 4, 5, 6. Repeat! Inhale. 1, 2, 3, 4. Hold it. 1, 2, 3, 4. Exhale. 1, 2, 3, 4, 5, 6. Take a moment. Take a breath. Ask yourself, "How am I feeling?"

Breathing is your most easily accessible, yet most underutilized stress reducer. Stop. That's worth reading again. Breathing is your *most easily accessible, yet most underutilized stress reducer.* Those eight words make a pretty powerful case for doing the 4–4–6 often. Breathing is so easy to access that we forget the instant stress-reducing powers it brings.

**Warning:** Please don't just do the 4–4–6 once or twice while reading this book. Practice the 4–4–6 like a Ninja!

Stuck in traffic? Time for a 4–4–6. Late for a meeting? Time for a 4–4–6. Immersed in a project? Time for a 4–4–6. Grocery shopping? Family outings? Cleaning out the fridge, walking the dog. … Just about any time is a good time for a 4–4–6. Give it a try now. Inhale, 1, 2, 3, 4. Hold it. 1, 2, 3, 4. Exhale. 1, 2, 3, 4, 5, 6.

---

## Take Action!

1. Remember to deep breathe using the 4–4–6.

2. Do it often. Practice like a Ninja!

3. Be aware of the peace and clarity it brings.

■ ■ ■

Dad always used to say, in life the key is to:

**Function in disaster, finish in style!**

*Ken Baldridge (the 4–4–6 helps you function)*

#DeepBreathingWorks

**P.S.** Air is free!

# 8

# THE OGIVE CURVE

**Q.** Have you ever had a rollercoaster of a day? Today perhaps?

**A.** Ogive (pronounced o-jive) management

# MANAGING THE UPS AND DOWNS OF YOUR DAY

Ogive is a curve in statistics. It's called a cumulative frequency curve. Monitoring your ogive can minimize, and even eliminate, your WAFs. There is positive ogive and negative ogive.

*Positive ogive* is when one point ascends to another and another to infinity.

*Negative ogive* is when one point descends to another and another to infinity.

I learned about ogive from my father. He said that life and work are like an ogive curve, so many ups and downs. If you plot on a graph all the positive and negative things that happen in your day, week, month, and year, you take them out of your mind, heart, and soul and put them on the graph (see Figure 8.1). Doing this makes it easier to monitor your feelings, so you don't get too up or too down. You discover

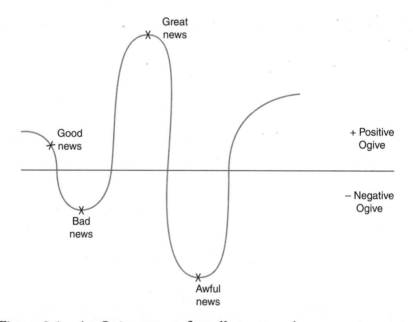

**Figure 8.1    An Ogive curve of a rollercoaster day.**

practical solutions. Situations and circumstances become more logical and less personal.

Dad always used to say, "There are no problems in life, just situations with an abundance of possible solutions." If you are experiencing a series of negative ogive events, you can feel your mood/spirit sinking down, down, down, and getting stuck in the quicksand of despair. If you experience too much negative upon negative, upon negative, you can become very depressed. Some are hospitalized for this depression. But if you are always, always, up, sometimes you're hospitalized, too!

You must watch your ogive! You can do this easily by asking yourself: "How's my ogive?" periodically throughout your day. To be more exacting, you can ask yourself, "On a scale of 1 to 10, 1 being the doldrums of despair and 10 being euphoria, how's my ogive?"

If you detect you are seeping into negative ogive because cumulatively you have had negative upon negative upon negative occur, you can detect the negative ogive curve forming, which allows you to deflect it.

*Detect and deflect* is a good phrase to keep in mind. As you detect yourself descending into the negative, you must do something positive to pull yourself out. It helps to have a list of a few things that make you exceedingly happy. Music may do it; calling someone you love or someone who is fun may do it! Taking a moment and a breath can do it.

A rollercoaster day is when you have so much going on at once that can cause your emotions to rise to great heights of elation and then freefall down to great depths of despair on this wild ride of work and life. Plotting these events as points on an ogive curve or graph (see Figure 8.2) helps you to take the emotion out of the situation and move into a practical, more balanced state of being.

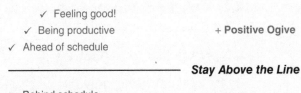

Figure 8.2    Plotting the ups and downs of your day on an ogive graph.

Remember that deep breathing can help you gain perspective when the ogive line starts to fall. Remember that breathing is your most easily accessible, most underutilized, stress reducer. It puts you in the present tense, it puts you in the now, and now is perfect. Test it any time. Because there is no time other than now, it makes sense to make the most of it.

You can rid yourself of your WAFs by watching your ogive. Monitoring your ogive will have a profound effect on your thoughts, decisions, and actions. Most importantly, it helps you acquire permanent access to the "House of Glad," which will be covered in the next chapter.

## Take Action!

1. Be aware of the ups and downs in your day.

2. Detect and deflect negativity to avoid descending into negative ogive.

3. Make a list of things that will help you ascend back to positive ogive.

■ ■ ■

**Tough times never last, but tough people do!**

*Robert Schuller, pastor and motivational speaker*

#NoNegativeOgiveAllowed

**P.S.** Watch your ogive!

# 9

# HOUSES OF MAD, GLAD, SAD, AND SCARED

**Q.** Ever wish there was a place you could go where you could feel happy and content more often?

**A.** There is. The House of Glad is the place. Here's how to get there....

There are four core human emotions and three of them rhyme. Mad, Glad, Sad, and Scared. I call them houses. So you have the House of Mad, the House of Glad, the House of Sad, and the House of Scared.

Ask yourself: "Which house do I live in most, and is it time to move?" When you ask yourself this question, you get the real answer. You feel it immediately. Most people do not live in the House of Glad. The most common answer is the House of Scared, followed by Mad and Sad, or Sad then Mad. Only a rare few report that they actually live in the House of Glad.

The good news is that, if you discover that you live in the House of Mad, Sad, or Scared, you have the capacity to move—right now!

Below are a few stories about the houses of human emotions, followed by concrete ways that you can make the House of Glad your primary residence.

## MACKENZIE'S STORY: GETTING TO GLAD

My daughter Mackenzie, at age 10, awoke and came in my bedroom very upset. She said she didn't want to go to school. I asked why she was so upset. She didn't want to tell me. I said it was OK to tell me, and she burst into tears and said, "I didn't finish my assignment and I am so afraid my reading teacher is going to be really mad at me." Mackenzie had never been afraid to go to school before, and now she was in the 5th grade, frightened to go.

I didn't know what to do. I loved her reading teacher, and so did she. She helped her immeasurably. So I called the school. The school administrative assistant answered. I said that Mackenzie was very upset. She asked what was wrong. I then asked, "Were you at the staff meeting I did for the faculty a few months ago, where I was speaking about the Four Houses of Human Emotion?"

"Yes!" she said.

I said, "Great! Here's what's happening. Mackenzie is in the House of Scared because she is afraid Ms. S. will be in the House of Mad, because she didn't finish a reading assignment. She is getting so scared it's making her move to the House of Sad, when all she really wants to do is live in the House of Glad!

Mary said, "We don't want sad and scared children at our school. Our school is a place for happy children who look forward to coming to school! So what you need me to do is to tell Ms. S. that Mackenzie is in the House of Sad because she is afraid Ms. S. will be in the House of Mad over an incomplete assignment, and that we want a big House of Glad welcome to school for Mackenzie this morning. Is that it?"

"YES! That's exactly it," I said.

She said, "Tell Mackenzie that everything will be alright. I will make sure Ms. S. doesn't get in the House of Mad over this. Please come in with Mackenzie. I will take care of it."

Mackenzie and I went to Ms. S.'s classroom and she was kneeling by the door with a huge smile on her face and her arms opened wide. She said, "Mackenzie come over here." Mackenzie ran into her arms. They shared a long hug.

I asked, "Mackenzie, what house are you in now?"

"The House of Glad mom!" They hugged again, and she went into the classroom with a smile and sigh of relief.

## SUSAN'S STORY: MOVING FROM A LIFE OF SCARED

Susan was a woman who attended a keynote presentation I gave in Charlotte, North Carolina, at a convention a few years ago. I was speaking about how when nothing is certain anything is possible. If you take fear out of your thought process, and develop and commit to a positive mindset that focuses on possibilities and solutions versus obstacles and problems. The theme of the meeting was, "Making the Best Even Better! Peak Performance Personified." I mentioned that living in the House of Scared creates an even more scary future because it's hard to escape fear when you constantly dwell on it. It can become all-consuming. A mind shift "move" to the House of Glad is essential for greater future success.

After the presentation, several people approached me to ask questions and thank me. I noticed one woman who stood to the side of the line, patiently waiting until everyone had gone. She shyly approached me and said her name was Susan and that I had no idea how much I had helped her. I thanked her and asked how. She proceeded to tell me that she was riddled with fear so much so that it was hard on her family. Her eyes started to tear up.

She told me, "When you were speaking, something just clicked! As you explained the houses model, I realized that I have been living in the Scared House far too long. The thought that I could move was new to me. I think things will be different from now on."

"How so?" I asked.

She said, "I have been diagnosed with clinical claustrophobia [a fear of being in closed or small spaces] and acute acrophobia [a fear of heights]. These fears have been running and ruining my life.

"How?" I asked.

"It's been awful!" she exclaimed. "For the past seven years I have not been able to ride on an elevator. Just the thought of entering an elevator makes me start to panic. I feel the heat of anxiety start to consume me, and I break out into a cold sweat. My husband and daughter have been hit the hardest by my chronic fearfulness. We haven't been able to go to Disney World as a family because I cannot stay in an enclosed car for more than a few minutes, and of course air travel has been unthinkable. My fears have been so bad that if there are no hotel rooms available on the first floor when we do staycations, we have to travel to another hotel where there is a ground floor room. My whole life revolves around my fears."

I have a degree in psychology and could empathize with Susan and really felt for her.

She went on to say, "But I think things will change now."

I asked how.

She said, "I don't exactly know, but I am willing to face my fears now. Will you help me do something?" Now I was feeling a bit of fear rising, thinking about what she could possibly want me to do.

"What?" I asked, as we walked across the sun-drenched atrium through the lobby, past the registration desks to the elevator bank. There were four elevators there. All were made of glass so you could see what was below, which was an unimaginable challenge for Susan as she would have to face both fears of tight spaces and heights all at once.

"Will you take an elevator ride with me?"

I said, "Sure! I'd love to! You realize they're made of glass?"

"I do," she said.

We popped in. She said, "the first floor please." I had her do the honors of pressing the button, and up we went. I could see the nervousness in her eyes. Seconds later the doors opened on the first floor and we jumped out. Susan started to laugh. Tears were streaming down her face. "You have no idea how incredible this is. You mentioned in your presentation that fear is 'false evidence appearing real.' That's so true. I did it!" she exclaimed! "I did it!! Let's go higher."

We got back into the elevator. This time there were other people in it. I asked her what floor. She replied, "The fifth." When we got out on the fifth floor Susan practically fell down laughing, saying, "I did it! I did it. Let's go higher!" She pushed the elevator call button. It came.

I asked, "Where to now?" She said 12! "All the way to the top?" I asked.

She said, "Yes! I'm ready."

As Susan pushed the button to take the elevator to the top, I turned to the people in the elevator and said, "You are witnessing history. This woman hasn't ridden in an elevator in over seven years!" They got out on the 8th floor. We got off on 12.

I said, "Congratulations!"

She said, "Let's go down to the lobby. I have to call my husband!" She pushed the button. The elevator doors opened. Susan stepped in and started laughing. She pressed the L button, and we got an express ride down to the lobby level. She walked into the lobby, called her husband, and said, "I did it!"

"Did what?" I could hear him ask.

"I rode in an elevator all the way to the top. Twelve flights."

Her daughter got on the phone. She started crying. "Our vacations are going to be a lot better from now on." Her daughter was crying, saying, "That's so great, mom!"

As we parted Susan said, "Thank you! Thanks for seeing this through with me. I think things really will be different from now on." I was amazed.

She made the move. She moved from the House of Scared, which instantly put her in the House of Glad. It was a marvel to be a part of her transition.

## My Story: The Missing Family Jewels or Visiting All the Houses at Once

My grandmother was very good at saving money. She knew the value of things as well. When she passed away, she left a magnificent diamond bracelet to me when I was 18. It had 18 one karat diamonds and 36 smaller diamonds. It was an inch wide all around and set in white gold. My mother said it was too ostentatious to wear out because it was so large. We kept it in a safe deposit box. Every couple of years, I would sign out the box, go to the private room, put on the bracelet, and admire it.

Years passed. Then a fancy occasion came around, a family wedding. I went to the safe deposit box. The name on the box number had changed. The key did not fit either. I was told that all was well. There must have been a mistake. When I called later, the bank officer said he was still looking into it. The House of Scared was starting to take hold.

I called again a few days later and was told the grim news. The payment for the safe deposit box had lapsed. The bank said they sent several notices. Unfortunately, those notices went to my previous address and were never forwarded. Despite my having the same phone number, no one bothered to call.

In the state of Connecticut if a safe deposit box is dormant for several years, they drill it open and sell the contents at auction. After further research, I found that's exactly what happened. Upon hearing this news, I moved quickly from the House of Scared to Sad. Sad to hear about the irrecoverable loss of a family heirloom that I thought my daughter would have one day. Then back to Scared when I realized I had to tell my mother what had happened. Then to the House of Mad for this happening in the first place. It was fascinating in retrospect how many houses my mind was racing in and out of due to this situation.

Nervously, I called my mother. I felt so irresponsible for losing the bracelet. I told her the bank had sold it at auction for a third of the value and that a check was being sent to me instead of the bracelet. I was worried about her reaction. What she said surprised me. She said, "That bracelet was too large and dangerous to wear. I always worried that if you wore it, some thief would hit you over the head with a bag of rocks or something and run off with it. You are much better off with the cash." Ha! That put me back in the House of Glad, my primary residence.

## ANOTHER JOY STORY: ATTACK FROM THE HOUSE OF MAD WOMAN

On my way home from the post office, I heard a loud car horn beeping furiously behind me. I hesitated, turning left across traffic because a truck was in front of me and I couldn't see the traffic light. That made the horn blast longer. As the arrow signal turned from green to yellow, I turned left and then swerved into a gas station to get away from this crazy, enraged woman, who was fast on my tail.

To my surprise, she turned into the gas station, too, pulled up next to me, and started screaming, her arms flailing. When she started to get out of her car, I wanted no part of it. I found an opening in the stream of morning traffic and bolted away. She followed me. I ducked into a side street to lose her. She couldn't get across the intersection fast enough to catch up to me. Relief! I had lost her.

Some might have yelled back. Not me. Not to say I wasn't tempted, but the House of Mad is a place I do not want to go. I have no interest in dwelling in the Mad House and want no part of. It was obvious from this brief encounter that she lived in the House of Mad. I find I have to protect my precious House of Glad lifestyle from people like her.

## MARY (MY ROCK) LOVES THE HOUSES

I told my best friend, Mary, about the Houses of Human Emotion. Because of this, we immediately started speaking the language. She asked if the House of Glad has rooms. I said, "Yes! But it also has levels, stairs, and an elevator, as do all the houses."

House of Glad behavior can be anything from calm delight on the ground floor to elation, euphoria, and overly zealous behavior on the top floors. The same for all the other houses. Ground floor in the House of Mad ranges from annoyed to angry. Enraged, livid, and furious are on the higher levels, as the feelings escalate. On the main floor of the House of Sad is sorrow and despair that can climb to dismal, distraught, and devastating depression. The House of Scared floors go from afraid and nervous up to panicky, horrified, and terrified.

Mary said, "I like our new lingo, because it is easier to express how we feel. It's a whole new way of talking that is more interesting, constructive, and practical than the old way. For instance, if I was having a bad day, I would typically tell you I was depressed and why. Now instead of saying I feel down, I say, 'I'm in the House of Sad at the moment,' and we laugh our way out of it, and then we start thinking of ways to get back to the House of Glad." Striving for Glad is a good and achievable goal.

Mary went on to say, "What helps the most is knowing that if you end up in a bad house, it's temporary (a state versus a trait), especially when you make the House of Glad the house you commit to, the house you go home to."

She also likes the R.E.N.T. concept. R.E.N.T. is the key to successful House of Glad living! R.E.N.T. is covered in the next chapter, but to give you a sneak preview, the expression I created to keep with the metaphor is, "To live in the House of Glad, you have to pay your R.E.N.T. every day."

R.E.N.T. stands for Rest, Exercise, Nutrition, and Thoughts. Mary said she likes the R.E.N.T. concept because it provides a solution for how to escape the less desirable houses you may find yourself in and gives you the power to return to the House of Glad.

Once I, surprisingly, found myself actually living in the House of Scared, despite being raised by optimistic parents in the House of Glad. I could tell I had somehow moved to the Scared House because I would awake feeling anxious, and a nervous feeling would stay with me day after day. Have you ever felt this way? When I realized that I was starting to live in the House of Scared, I thought, "How could this be?" It was during the recession and I was spending too much money on shoes and such things, and it got to be too much. Have you ever had an out-of-money experience? Once I detected that I was living in the House of Scared, I decided to move back to the House of Glad. You can do it, too.

## Conclusion

What the stories in this chapter demonstrate is that you will experience all kinds of emotions in your life. Things will happen that you don't expect that can throw you into a state of Mad, Glad, Sad, and/ or Scared. The point is, you have the power to declare where your primary residence is, the place to go home to. Of course, being human, you will find yourself in a variety of houses every day, depending on the situation. The point is to make the House of Glad your primary residence, the place to call home, the place to go back to regardless of circumstances.

Each House of Human Emotion comes with its own set of challenges. You end up living in the house where you "dwell" most. Do you know anyone who dwells upon sad things? They tell you sad stories, say how sad everything is. Or maybe you know someone who lives in the Mad House. People who live in the Mad House are angry about everything. Nothing is ever quite right or good enough. They actually *look* for things to be angry about. Recently, I met a man who said he lives in the House of Mad and he is happy there. He likes it when he gets riled up. It makes him feel alive. Mad to him is adrenaline and passion, and it works for him, which is fine with me as long as I don't have to live with him in the Mad House.

It takes just as much work to live in the House of Glad as it does to live in all the other houses. You must fix the roof, pull the weeds, and work at being and staying happy. But what's the alternative? When sad, mad, and scared are the other choices, I'd choose glad every time. Wouldn't you?

## Take Action!

1. Watch for the house you end up in when things don't go as expected in your day.

2. Remind yourself that you can move to the House of Glad any time you wish.

3. Make a list of things that make you truly happy, and do some of these things to help you move back home to Glad.

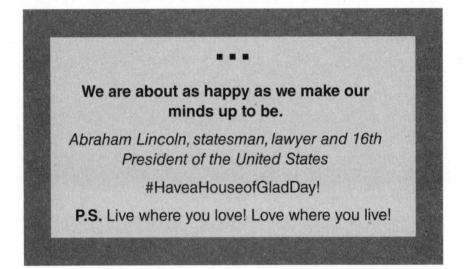

**■ ■ ■**

**We are about as happy as we make our minds up to be.**

*Abraham Lincoln, statesman, lawyer and 16th President of the United States*

#HaveaHouseofGladDay!

**P.S.** Live where you love! Love where you live!

# 10

# PAY YOUR
# R.E.N.T. EVERY
# DAY!

**Q.** How do you live in the House of Glad?

**A.** You must pay your R.E.N.T. every day!

# Rest, Exercise, Nutrition, and Thoughts

R.E.N.T. stands for rest, exercise, nutrition, and thoughts.

To live in the House of Glad, you must pay your R.E.N.T. every day! If you blow the R.E.N.T., you may find yourself evicted from the House of Glad and living in less desirable conditions. Think about this for a minute. How do you feel when you are tired? What happens to your thoughts, your actions? Most people when tired find that it takes two or three times longer to do something and they make three to five more mistakes. This does not make for a House of Glad experience! What about lack of exercise? Do you ever start to feel sluggish when you get too busy or lazy to exercise? What about nutrition? What choices do you make on how to fuel your body? Your thoughts need to be fueled as well.

Let's dissect the R.E.N.T. formula to see how it can best work for you. Your emotional and physical well-being start with rest.

## REST

*"The amount of rest required for most people is 5 minutes more!"*

What happens to you when you're tired? Do you become upset easily? Feel overwhelmed? Anxious? Frustrated? Rest is one of the most important factors in living a House of Glad life. Here are three ways to get the rest that leads to greater future success:

1. **Take a Purple Break.** As explained in detail in Chapter 1, the Purple Break is a quick and practical way to rejuvenate. It's when you take a moment. Relax and breathe. Close and then cover your eyes. Doing this restores the visual purple, also known as rhodopsin, in your eyes that breaks down in bright light, causing fatigue. It is restored in total darkness. Begin your Purple Break with a backwards count from any number you wish. If pressed for time, start at 15. On each breath you take, go to the next number.

Such as, 15, exhale, inhale, 14, exhale and so on. At the Baldridge Learning Center we also call it the "Blackout Countdown." We do them several times throughout the day to stay focused and positive regardless of circumstance. They only take a minute, and the payoff is huge!

**Warning:** You have to be careful when taking your Purple Breaks because most people don't know what they are. If people you work with see you with your head in your hands, the nonverbal message is typically perceived that there is a terrible problem or that things are not good. This especially problematic if you are in finance, HR or the head of the department or company. This is how rumors start.

Ha! So be careful to be discrete when taking your Purple Break, unless you let others in on what it is, and then take them wherever and whenever you wish.

2. **Practice the 4–4–6.** The 4–4–6 was explained in Chapter 7. It is a great way to feel more rested through oxygenation. Infusing your lungs and cells with deeper oxygen intake creates calmness, followed by an energy lift. Have you done the 4–4–6 since you read about it earlier in this book? The key is not to simply know about the 4–4–6. It's to use it daily like a Ninja! Inhale, 1, 2, 3, 4, hold it, 1, 2, 3, 4, exhale, 1, 2, 3, 4, 5, 6. Repeat, repeat, repeat!

**Warning:** Be careful not to exhale too forcefully because a loud, big exhale can be perceived as a sigh of defeat, discouragement, or frustration. You don't want to make the wrong impression. Also, a heavy exhale on the phone is not a good idea, for obvious reasons.

3. **Ask a Question.** Take a breath, take a moment, ask a question. By taking a deep, conscious breath, you place yourself in the present. Taking a moment helps you to regroup. It allows for clarity of thought to resurface. Asking yourself "What's the priority?" or "How am I feeling?" gets you back in tune with yourself and what needs to be accomplished. It helps you regain focus to make the best use of your time.

**Warning:** It's human nature to make statements rather than ask questions—statements like "I'm so overwhelmed," "I don't know where to begin," or "I'm exhausted." This self-talk is self-defeating and counter-productive, so be sure to ask questions instead of falling into the trap of making exasperating statements.

## EXERCISE

My friend Jordon is an exercise fanatic. Do you know people like him? He goes to the gym for two hours every day for a vigorous workout. He is always quite amused each January when the gym becomes packed with the New Year's resolution people in their fancy new gym clothes, only to find in February the gym is back to the regulars who have made a consistent and concerted commitment to their exercise habit.

To exercise habitually takes planning. One person told me he sleeps in his workout sweats so he can just roll out of bed and run out the door to the gym or take part in his daily running route. I took his advice, and it worked! Now I sleep in sweats, wake up, and run out into the morning.

Many people are quite hard on themselves about exercise. The guilt of not doing it. The false promises of tomorrow for sure! Taking small steps works well here. My dad wanted to run. He was definitely not a runner. He decided one day to just run from our mailbox to the mailbox next door. That was it! The following day he ran past the first mailbox to the second. And so on. Within a year he registered for a marathon in Marathon, Florida. He didn't win, didn't even finish. He made it to 13.2 miles before flagging down the bus that picked up depleted runners. He was pleased about his progress since that first day running from mailbox to mailbox.

What small steps can you take today that will further your success toward a steady exercise routine?

When I speak at conventions, I say to the audience, "Raise your hands in the air like you don't care!" [A line from an old disco song from the 1980s] Hundreds, sometimes thousands of hands go up and sway back and forth. Then I say, "I call that exercise! Check it off your list! I'm so tired of people feeling guilty for not exercising. It doesn't take much to just move!" This comment is usually followed by uproarious laughter because it is so true. We beat ourselves up for not getting to the gym and sticking to an exercise routine, when it's so simple to just park the car far, take the stairs more often, or perhaps sleep in your workout clothes and run out the door as soon as you roll out of bed.

I recently saw comedian Jacob Williams on a late night talk show describing his workout plan. He said his workout plan is sitting on the couch and hoping things will work out. That made me laugh. I've done that. Have you?

So don't just sit there: do something! Get up, get out, and keep moving! Do you realize that your next workout is as close as your smart phone? Simply search YouTube for your next yoga, Pilates, planks, cardio, weight lifting, kick boxing workout. It's all there, every kind of workout you could ever want, and virtually thousands of different ways to do them.

I know you know this. But do you do it? Knowing and doing are two very different things. So put this book down, give me 20 push-ups, 25 jumping jacks, and 30 squats. Stat! Or search YouTube for the exercise of your choice. I have a river in the backyard and always dreamed of doing yoga by the river. One day I made it a reality by simply searching for yoga routines and clicked and let the sun salutations begin!

**Warning:** Be sure to check with your doctor and personal trainer before changing any physical activity. Hasty, impulsive, new exercise regimes can lead to injuries that can happen incredibly quickly, with a recovery that seems endless.

## NUTRITION

Joann Flynn is a nutritionist and friend who has a wealth of knowledge about healthy eating. I asked her for some quick, impactful advice about what to eat to get the best payoff.

I asked: "What's the healthiest vegetable?" (I am a seafood eating vegetarian who hates vegetables, so I must eat a vegetable that pays off.) Her first thought was broccoli, followed by rich, dark, greens. (Yes, kale fits in this category for you kale fanatics.)

Then I asked: "What's the worst thing you can eat?" Quickly, without missing a beat, she said, "Sugar." She went on to say that sugar was evil, and it is in everything! Joann explained that sugar is more addictive than nicotine or heroin. My conclusion is that broccoli is good, and sugar is evil. (I like to keep it simple.)

Dr. Mercola wrote an article titled "The Truth About Sugar Addiction: 76 Ways Sugar Can Ruin Your Health." (Am I the only one who sees the irony of the doctor having the word "cola" in his name?! A can of cola contains 39 grams of sugar.)

In his article he categorizes the 76 ways sugar can ruin your health into four groups:

- **Nutrient Imbalance or Deficiency.** Bad cholesterol levels, lowers vitamin E, body changes sugar into fat in the bloodstream.

- **Behavioral Changes.** Emotional instability, difficulty concentrating, hyperactivity.

- **Increased Risk of Disease.** Feeds cancer cells, increases systolic blood pressure, obesity, dizziness, food allergies, gum disease, tooth decay, emphysema, and headaches.

- **Bodily Impairments.** Suppression of the immune system, premature aging, change in protein structure, dehydration, hormonal imbalances, unclear thinking, fluid retention.

I repeat: Sugar is evil.

Joann also recommended that people include protein in their diet for energy. Many think that carbs drive energy, which they do, but only temporarily. Joann explained, "Protein it is like a log on a fire. It smolders and lasts a very long time. Eating carbohydrates for energy is like putting paper or kindling on a fire. It provides instant flames, but burns out very quickly, causing a quick, but unsustainable energy boost. The bottom line on nutrition is to make it easy to eat foods that are good for you. The more convenient foods tend to be the most detrimental, so stock up on healthy grab-and-go foods.

**Hint:** Joann mentioned that you can combine a protein with a fruit to create a nice, healthy balance, such as nuts and raisins. Remember to choose wisely before eating anything. Healthy eating and living ultimately involves (1) taking the time to prepare to eat healthy and (2) making the choice to actually eat the healthier foods you buy. Don't eat late at night is more food for thought!

## THE LENT STORY

After interviewing Joann Flynn about healthy eating tips and learning that broccoli was good and sugar was evil, I decided to eat more broccoli and give up sugar for Lent. I tend to share my goals to have more accountability for them, so I told my son Wilson, who was seven at the time, "There is a ritual called Lent, where you give up something for 40 days and 40 nights that you really, really, love. I really, really love sugar, so I'm giving it up. No more cookies, candy, or cake for me," I proclaimed. "What do you really, really, love that you're going to give up?" I asked.

Wilson said, "I really, really, love church!" Ha! I didn't see that one coming!

It was really difficult to give up refined sugar (bad sugars, like cookies and candy) for so long. The cravings were real and luring, but I resisted. Substituting the good sugars (such as fruit) for the bad helped. Eventually, I felt great. Getting through the first week to 10 days was the hardest part. It took every ounce of determination, discipline, and will power I had.

My recommendation is to watch the amount of bad sugar you take in. "Good sugar comes in healthy whole food, while bad sugars come in highly refined, processed foods," according to Sandi Busch a professional health writer specializing in web content for physicians, hospitals, and professional organizations, in an article titled, "Good & Bad Sugars" in SFGate.com Healthy Eating.

**Bottom Line:** Eat your veggies and your protein. Reduce your sugar and you will have easy access to the House of Glad!

## THOUGHTS

What do you say when you talk to yourself? Are you hard on yourself? People tend to be harder on themselves than they would ever be on others and say negative and demanding things to themselves that they would never say to anyone! Have you ever caught yourself saying things like, "Why did I wait so long to start this?" or "How stupid of me to do that!" It's important to be kind to yourself. Say nice things! Often, we don't have nice things to say to ourselves at the ready. It's not natural for most people tell themselves that they are doing a good job. Sue at the Stop & Shop is an exception:

## DAMN I'M GOOD

Sue at the local Stop & Shop always wears a button on her lapel that says, "Damn I'm Good!" She has worn it so long it is beginning to rust around the edges. Sue is an older woman who has been through a lot of tough times with family and personal illness, but she is always at the store with her button on, working hard bagging the groceries or ringing the register.

Once I asked her, "Hey, Sue, are you good?!" She quickly and emphatically replied, "No! I'm Damn Good!"

If you were to say something good to yourself, what would you say? Most have no idea.

## GREETING CARD

I saw a birthday greeting card that had two women sitting side-by-side at the beauty salon. One said to the other, "You look great! Have you lost weight? Love your outfit." Then she tuned to her friend and said, "Your turn!" This type of banter is bound to up your Ogive, thus keeping you in the House of Glad.

## FLOODING

Émile Coué, French apothecary, inventor, and philosopher is the father of *autosuggestion* (another word for self-hypnosis), self-mastery thought consciousness, and the placebo effect. Coué would write the following phrase on a prescription pad and give it to patients. It would make sick people healthier and poor people wealthier:

*"Every day in every way I am getting better and better."*

He would prescribe that his patients say this phrase 20 times each morning upon rising and 20 times each night before drifting off to sleep.

I gave this idea a try and found that it works! Each day that goes by, you start looking for ways to make things better in your life. Give this ritual a try for 30 days and see what happens.

Coué calls this repetition *flooding*. If you say it once, it has little effect, but by saying it over and over when you first wake up and when you doze off to sleep, you will begin to reprogram your thoughts.

The rare time that most people unconsciously do flooding is when nervous. They tell themselves how nervous they are as in, "I'm so nervous, I'm so nervous." Or when tired, as in, "I'm so tired! I'm so tired, I'm so incredibly tired!" Negative flooding is counterproductive and can lead to depression and illness.

So what can you say in addition to the better and better model Coué recommends? I Try flooding "I am a hot potato!" 20 times each morning and night and see what happens. If all else fails, I guarantee you'll laugh! I am a hot potato means that you are super-cool.

My Swedish friend Sig said upon hearing this, "Joy, I think you are a sweet potato." I like that.

## R.E.N.T. Validity

Seeking validation regarding my R.E.N.T. Theory, I asked Dr. Jonas McAlarney, a physician in emergency medicine, about the houses and the R.E.N.T. concept. He said it made good sense. "Why?" I asked.

He said, "Most people come to the Emergency Room because they have blown the R.E.N.T. Right? They are not resting, not exercising, not eating right, and certainly not thinking right."

I told him that some people undervalue the importance of thoughts, the T in R.E.N.T. and think of it as psychobabble. I asked what he thought about that.

Dr. McAlarney said, "*The T is the most important part of R.E.N.T.!*" When I asked why, he said, "Because your thoughts drive everything!" He went on to say: "Your thoughts are what make you decide to pay or blow the R.E.N.T. They make you decide whether to rest, exercise, or eat right. Your thoughts make all the difference."

## Take Action!

1. Make a commitment to pay your R.E.N.T. every day!

2. Have a R.E.N.T. buddy. Hold each other accountable. It's even more fun to share the R.E.N.T.

3. Divide and conquer. Start small and build healthy daily habits.

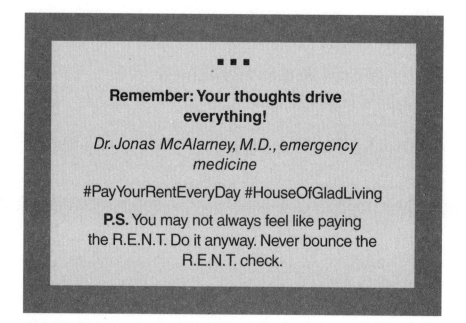

■ ■ ■

**Remember: Your thoughts drive everything!**

*Dr. Jonas McAlarney, M.D., emergency medicine*

#PayYourRentEveryDay #HouseOfGladLiving

**P.S.** You may not always feel like paying the R.E.N.T. Do it anyway. Never bounce the R.E.N.T. check.

# 11

# MORE ON FLOODING

**Q.** Does saying positive words to yourself over and over really work?

**A.** Yes!

Flooding positive affirmations will improve your mood and increase your productivity and profitability. Moods change. The more you can positively influence your mindset, the more your business will thrive. This chapter is dedicated to providing you with a variety of ways to practice the art of flooding. The goal is to master it. Consciously flooding your mind with positive thoughts when idle will build positive thought momentum. Idle times means when waiting, driving, walking somewhere, or arriving early for a meeting. These are all perfect times to practice the concept of flooding. Flooding pushes out worry, anxiety, fear, and doubt and fills your mind with positivity.

Most people don't flood positive messages to themselves because they don't know what to say. To start the flooding habit, find the phrases you like below and read them aloud. Say them 20 or 30 times twice a day for 30 days. Watch for the magic to appear.

## ÉMILE COUÉ

Every day, in every way, I'm getting better and better.

Every day, in every way, I'm getting better and better. Every day, in every way, I'm getting better and better. Every day, in every way, I'm getting better and better. Every day, in every way, I'm getting better and better. Every day, in every way, I'm getting better and better. Every day, in every way, I'm getting better and better. Every day, in every way, I'm getting better and better. Every day, in every way, I'm getting better and better. Every day, in every way, I'm getting better and better. Every day, in every way, I'm getting better and better. Every day, in every way, I'm getting better and better. Every day, in every way, I'm getting better and better. Every day, in every way, I'm getting better and better. Every day, in every way, I'm getting better and better. Every day, in every way, I'm getting better and better. Every day, in every way, I'm getting better and better. Every day, in every way, I'm getting better and better. Every day, in every way, I'm getting better and better. Every day, in every way, I'm getting better and better. Every day, in every way, I'm getting better and better. Every day, in every way, I'm getting better and better. Every day, in every way, I'm getting better and better. Every day, in every way, I'm getting better and better. Every day, in every way, I'm getting better and better. Every day, in every way, I'm getting better and better. Every day, in every way, I'm getting better and better. Every day, in every way, I'm getting better and better. Every day, in every way, I'm getting better and better. Every day, in every way, I'm getting better and better. Every day, in every way, I'm getting better and better. Every day, in every way, I'm getting better and better. Every day, in every way, I'm getting better and better. Every day, in every way, I'm getting better and better. Every day, in every way, I'm getting better and better.

Dr. Norman Vincent Peale recommends adding these five words to any affirmation: "And I do believe that!"

Example: "Every day, in every way, I am getting better and better. *And I do believe that!*"

I have personally found that those five extra words make a big difference because they challenge your belief system that may be secretly saying things like, "Why are you saying these superfluous affirmations? They won't work."

## ROBERT ADAMS

All is well, all is well, all is perfectly well and unfolding
as it should.

All is well, all is well, all is perfectly well and unfolding as it should. All is well, all is well, all is perfectly well and unfolding as it should. All is well, all is well, all is perfectly well and unfolding as it should. All is well, all is well, all is perfectly well and unfolding as it should. All is well, all is well, all is perfectly well and unfolding as it should. All is well, all is well, all is perfectly well and unfolding as it should. All is well, all is well, all is perfectly well and unfolding as it should. All is well, all is well, all is perfectly well and unfolding as it should. All is well, all is well, all is perfectly well and unfolding as it should. All is well, all is well, all is perfectly well and unfolding as it should. All is well, all is well, all is perfectly well and unfolding as it should. All is well, all is well, all is perfectly well and unfolding as it should. All is well, all is well, all is perfectly well and unfolding as it should. All is well, all is well, all is perfectly well and unfolding as it should. All is well, all is well, all is perfectly well and unfolding as it should. All is well, all is well, all is perfectly well and unfolding as it should. All is well, all is well, all is perfectly well and unfolding as it should. All is well, all is well, all is perfectly well and unfolding as it should. All is well, all is well, all is perfectly well and unfolding as it should. All is well, all is well, all is perfectly well and unfolding as it should. All is well, all is well, all is perfectly well and unfolding as it should. All is well, all is well, all is perfectly well and unfolding as it should. All is well, all is well, all is perfectly well and unfolding as it should. All is well, all is well, all is perfectly well and unfolding as it should. All is well, all is well, all is perfectly well and unfolding as it should. All is well, all is well, all is perfectly well and unfolding as it should.

*AND I DO BELIEVE THAT!*

## Norman Vincent Peale

I expect the best and I get the best.

I expect the best and I get the best, I expect the best and I get the best. I expect the best and I get the best. I expect the best and I get the best. I expect the best and I get the best, I expect the best and I get the best. I expect the best and I get the best. I expect the best and I get the best. I expect the best and I get the best, I expect the best and I get the best. I expect the best and I get the best. I expect the best and I get the best. I expect the best and I get the best, I expect the best and I get the best. I expect the best and I get the best. I expect the best and I get the best. I expect the best and I get the best, I expect the best and I get the best. I expect the best and I get the best. I expect the best and I get the best. I expect the best and I get the best, I expect the best and I get the best. I expect the best and I get the best. I expect the best and I get the best. I expect the best and I get the best, I expect the best and I get the best. I expect the best and I get the best. I expect the best and I get the best. I expect the best and I get the best, I expect the best and I get the best. I expect the best and I get the best. I expect the best and I get the best. I expect the best and I get the best, I expect the best and I get the best. I expect the best and I get the best. I expect the best and I get the best. I expect the best and I get the best, I expect the best and I get the best. I expect the best and I get the best. I expect the best and I get the best. I expect the best and I get the best, I expect the best and I get the best. I expect the best and I get the best. I expect the best and I get the best. I expect the best and I get the best, I expect the best and I get the best. I expect the best and I get the best. I expect the best and I get the best.

*AND I DO BELIEVE THAT!*

## LOUISE HAY

Someone somewhere is looking for exactly what you
have to offer.

Someone somewhere is looking for exactly what you have to offer.
Someone somewhere is looking for exactly what you have to offer.
Someone somewhere is looking for exactly what you have to offer.
Someone somewhere is looking for exactly what you have to offer.
Someone somewhere is looking for exactly what you have to offer.
Someone somewhere is looking for exactly what you have to offer.
Someone somewhere is looking for exactly what you have to offer.
Someone somewhere is looking for exactly what you have to offer.
Someone somewhere is looking for exactly what you have to offer.
Someone somewhere is looking for exactly what you have to offer.
Someone somewhere is looking for exactly what you have to offer.
Someone somewhere is looking for exactly what you have to offer.
Someone somewhere is looking for exactly what you have to offer.
Someone somewhere is looking for exactly what you have to offer.
Someone somewhere is looking for exactly what you have to offer.
Someone somewhere is looking for exactly what you have to offer.
Someone somewhere is looking for exactly what you have to offer.
Someone somewhere is looking for exactly what you have to offer.
Someone somewhere is looking for exactly what you have to offer.
Someone somewhere is looking for exactly what you have to offer.
Someone somewhere is looking for exactly what you have to offer.
Someone somewhere is looking for exactly what you have to offer.
Someone somewhere is looking for exactly what you have to offer.
Someone somewhere is looking for exactly what you have to offer.
Someone somewhere is looking for exactly what you have to offer.

*AND I DO BELIEVE THAT!*

## JOY BALDRIDGE

I am a hot potato!

I am a hot potato! I am a hot potato! I am a hot potato. I am a hot
potato! I am a hot potato! I am a hot potato! I am a hot potato! I am
a hot potato! I am a hot potato! I am a hot potato! I am a hot potato!

I am a hot potato! I am a hot potato! I am a hot potato! I am a hot potato! I am a hot potato! I am a hot potato! I am a hot potato! I am a hot potato! I am a hot potato! I am a hot potato! I am a hot potato! I am a hot potato! I am a hot potato! I am a hot potato! I am a hot potato! I am a hot potato! I am a hot potato! I am a hot potato! I am a hot potato! I am a hot potato! I am a hot potato! I am a hot potato! I am a hot potato! I am a hot potato! I am a hot potato! I am a hot potato! I am a hot potato! I am a hot potato! I am a hot potato! I am a hot potato! I am a hot potato! I am a hot potato! I am a hot potato! I am a hot potato! I am a hot potato! I am a hot potato! I am a hot potato! I am a hot potato! I am a hot potato! I am a hot potato! I am a hot potato! I am a hot potato! I am a hot potato! I am a hot potato! I am a hot potato! I am a hot potato! I am a hot potato! I am a hot potato! I am a hot potato! I am a hot potato! I am a hot potato! I am a hot potato! I am a hot potato! I am a hot potato! I am a hot potato! I am a hot potato! I am a hot potato! I am a hot potato! I am a hot potato! I am a hot potato! I am a hot potato! I am a hot potato! I am a hot potato! I am a hot potato! I am a hot potato! I am a hot potato! I am a hot potato! I am a hot potato! I am a hot potato! I am a hot potato! I am a hot potato!

*AND I DO BELIEVE THAT!*

Write your own words or favorite slogan to flood here:

_____

_____

_____


*AND I DO BELIEVE THAT!*

To review: Flooding is saying the same phrase 20 to 30 times in a row. Listen to what you say when you talk to yourself. It may be the perfect time to change it up and convert it to one of the phrases above instead. Remember: Flooding is autosuggestion, also referred to as self-hypnosis. Change your thinking and you change your life.

## Take Action!

1. Determine what is most important for you to improve.

2. Select one of the flooding sayings or create your own.

3. Give flooding a try. See how it can work for you.

■ ■ ■

**When starting my business, a friend suggested I flood these words:**

*Walk with confidence in the direction of your dreams, act as though it were impossible to fail.*

**This quote was inspired by the words of Henry David Thoreau and Dorothea Brande, both renowned American writers.**

**It worked.**

**So did this one....**

*I am a hot potato.*

#FloodingWorks

**P.S.** At first flooding may seem cliché or silly like the old *Saturday Night Live* sketch. Do it anyway.

**Side note:** A friend of mine went to a hypnotist to stop smoking. When she left his office, she muttered, "Well, that was a complete waste of time and money!" as she was pulling her cigarette pack out of her purse and tossing it, along with her lighter, into the nearest trash receptacle.

# 12

# R.E.N.T. ASSESSMENT

**Q.** Can you pay your R.E.N.T. every day?

**A.** Yes! If you keep it top of mind and take assessments.

To take a deeper dive into evaluating your R.E.N.T., answer the questions below in each category. This will help you determine where you can improve the most to have a happier and more productive work life by paying your R.E.N.T. every day.

## REST ASSESSMENT

1. Do you take breaks in your day?
2. Do you become upset easily when tired?
3. Do you make more mistakes when tired?
4. Do you feel tired a lot?
5. Do you wish you were sleeping now?
6. What gives you the most energy?
7. How much caffeine do you drink?
8. What's one thing you can do to further your success with rest? (Take Purple Breaks perhaps?)
9. What do you need to stop doing to feel more rested?
10. What will you think, feel, and do when you have more energy?

## EXERCISE ASSESSMENT

1. Do you enjoy a particular form of exercise?
2. Do you have an exercise routine?
3. Do you stretch before exercising?
4. Do you benchmark to measure your progress with an exercise tracker such as a Fitbit, Apple Watch, a pedometer, or a fitness app?
5. Do you find that exercise alleviates stress?
6. What's one thing you can do to further your success with exercise?
7. What do you need to stop doing to get into better shape?
8. What modifications can you make to achieve greater results from exercise?
9. What is your ultimate exercise goal?
10. What will you think, feel, and do when you reach your exercise goals?

## NUTRITION ASSESSMENT

1. Do you make good choices about what to eat throughout the day and minimize/avoid foods that are unhealthy?
2. Do you drink 8 to 10 eight-ounce glasses of water each day?
3. Do you eat after 7:00 p.m.?
4. What triggers you to make unhealthy eating choices?
5. Are you happy with your weight? What is the best weight range for you?
6. What's one thing you can do to further your success with your nutrition?
7. What do you need to stop doing to create better nutritional habits?
8. What modifications can you make to achieve greater results in nutrition?
9. What is your ultimate nutrition goal?
10. What will you think, feel, and do once you reach your nutrition goal?

## THOUGHTS ASSESSMENT

1. Do you typically think positive or negative thoughts?
2. Do you read inspirational materials and positive quotes?
3. Do you write your thoughts down in a journal or keep a gratitude list?
4. What do you do to lift yourself up when feeling down?
5. Do you practice mindfulness by being in the here and now?
6. What is one thing you can do to further your success with your thoughts?
7. What's one thing you should stop doing to better nurture your thoughts?
8. What modifications can you make to achieve greater results in the way you think?
9. What is your ultimate mindset goal?
10. What will you think, feel, and do once you've reached it?

## Take Action!

1. Take the above assessments from time to time to stay on track with your physical and mental health goals.

2. Divide and conquer. Select one R.E.N.T. area to focus on at a time.

3. Use the buddy system to stay disciplined and stick to your R.E.N.T regime.

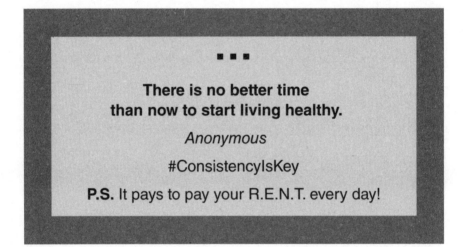

■ ■ ■

**There is no better time
than now to start living healthy.**

*Anonymous*

#ConsistencyIsKey

**P.S.** It pays to pay your R.E.N.T. every day!

# 13

# WHAT'S YOUR "ONE THING"?

**Q.** How do you take your career to greater heights?

**A.** Focus on the "One Thing."

I hosted a cable TV talk show, *At Work with Joy Baldridge*, for several years. I interviewed CEOs of Fortune 500 companies like IBM, Pepsi, PerkinElmer, and Time Mirror about how they made it to the top.

One of my favorite responses was from CEO Bill Rowe, who was in publishing. When I asked what he did along the way to rise to the top, he modestly said he wasn't smarter or more talented than others, but he did do something that he felt made a difference. He said he asked himself a question, 220 business days a year for 10 years, and that's what advanced his career to the C-suite.

I asked, "What was the question?"

He said: "What's the one thing I can do to further my success for tomorrow?" Then he would do that one thing, and leave his office feeling satisfied. He said that a lot of people leave dissatisfied, staying late and struggling to do more and more. By focusing on the "one thing" that leads to further success each day, he created a powerful momentum of incremental gains that was built over time. The key is to do it consistently.

Now that Part 1 of this book is coming to an end, it would be a good idea to reflect on what you have read. Take a moment and flip back through the pages and note below the "golden nuggets" you would like to use before moving on to Part 2. Is it the Purple Break, AFA All the Way, Function in Disaster, Finish in Style, Salt the Hay, Find a Way, Say Goodbye to Your WAFs, Now Is Perfect, 4–4–6 Breathing, the Ogive Curve, House of Glad, Paying Your R.E.N.T., or Flooding? Once your list is complete, rank the top three things you will do differently, and commit to doing your "one thing" today.

**Favorite Golden Nuggets**

My top three Golden Nuggets in order of importance:

1. _____

2. _____

3. _____

The "one thing" I will commit to do first is:

_____

_____

## Take Action!

1. Ask yourself each business day: "What's the one thing I can do to further my success for tomorrow?"
2. Do it!
3. Leave your day feeling satisfied!

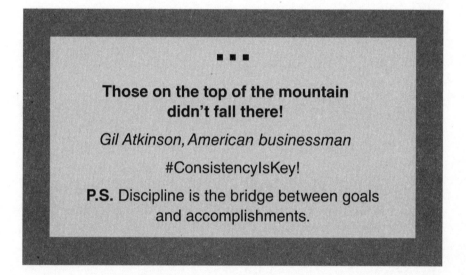

**. . .**

### Those on the top of the mountain didn't fall there!

*Gil Atkinson, American businessman*

#ConsistencyIsKey!

**P.S.** Discipline is the bridge between goals and accomplishments.

# PART 2

# 14

# THE VELVET HAMMER

**Q.** How can you find the best words to say when giving feedback?

**A.** Apply the Velvet Hammer.

The Velvet Hammer is a choice of words that are soft and smooth like velvet, yet pack a punch like a hammer and get results. They are useful in so many ways. They work effectively in management to deliver corrective feedback with ease, in sales to follow up or ask for the business without seeming pushy or rude, in meetings to make a comment that may go against the status quo, even at home with friends and family. Many combinations of words can be used to deliver a potentially difficult message with ease. My favorites are "Noticed and Wondering" and "Likelihood and When?"

"Noticed and Wondering" opens the conversation, "Likelihood and When" closes it. In psychology the *primacy effect* is the first impression you give, as in primary, meaning first. The *recency effect* is the last, or most recent, impression you give. One client at a major investment firm said that he has spent years working on making a good first impression, never realizing he had to make a good last impression as well.

Keep in mind that in addition to providing corrective feedback, the Velvet Hammer can be used for providing positive feedback as well. Below are a few examples of the Velvet Hammer words in action.

**Management Application Delivering Corrective and Positive Feedback**

> **Corrective Feedback:** "I *noticed* that you have been off schedule on the project lately, and I was *wondering* what's the **likelihood** that you can get back on track, and **when** might that be?"
>
> **Positive Feedback:** "I *noticed* that you have been generating and implementing some great new ideas, and I was *wondering* how you do it?"

**Sales Application with Prospects to Reconnect and Further the Sales Process**

> **Follow-up:** "I *noticed* it's been a while since we last spoke, and I was **wondering** when the best time would be to reconnect."
>
> **Closing Sales Appointments:** "I *noticed* in my notes from our last meeting that you were interested in having your partner join us

next time. I was *wondering* what the ***likelihood*** is of setting that up and *when* the best timing would be?"

**Closing the Sale:** What's the likelihood we can get budget approval? When might that be?

## Sales Application Providing Feedback to Top Producers

**Positive Observations:** "I *noticed* that your sales have increased by 40% over last year and was *wondering* whether you could share some of your new business development strategies with the team.

**Comment to Close More Sales:** "What's the ***likelihood*** of you closing the KMP business, and **when** might that be?"

## Internal Meeting Application

**Making a Comment:** "I *noticed* that we haven't discussed the financial implications of the merger, and I was *wondering* what your thoughts are on that."

**Positive Observation:** "I *noticed* that our employee engagement numbers are up, and I was *wondering* what has led to this great change?" "What's the **likelihood** we can keep going in this positive direction and **when** can we meet to monitor it?"

## Friend Application

**Making a Comment:** "I *noticed* that there's an exhibit at the museum, and I was *wondering* if you would like to go. **W**hen *are you free?*"

**Positive Observation:** "I've *noticed* how dedicated you have been to getting into better shape, and I was *wondering* what changes you have been making to your exercise routine?"

## Family Application

**Making a Comment:** "I *noticed* the dishes in the sink and I was *wondering* if you were going to do them tonight." ☺ **OR** "I *noticed* that you have been a bit abrupt when we speak, and I was *wondering* if you can be a little more kind and patient with me." (This works well with teenagers.)

**Positive Observation:** "I *noticed* you have been doing your homework as soon as you get home from school, and I was *wondering* how things are going."

Can you see how applying the Velvet Hammer can help you deliver a difficult conversation with more ease, as well as give positive feedback?

On my list of 10 most important characteristics of highly effective leaders, providing immediate feedback is the one characteristic that seems to be over-looked and most often avoided. Many people tend to be conflict adverse. Are you?

Some have no problem providing corrective feedback, but when it's done too harshly it can have consequences, too. Typically, when management feedback is delivered too harshly, the recipient calls in sick the next day, avoids the boss, or may even quit in retaliation.

When feedback is delayed, I call this the "spinach on your teeth" syndrome. If you have spinach on your teeth, do you want to know or not? It's still there. When something needs to be said, most people in the organization know it. Everyone, that is, except the person who needs the feedback. It's like someone walking around the office with a "kick me" sign on his or her back.

When feedback is not given in a timely manner, it can negatively impact productivity, morale, and the bottom line. If you have the expectation that you want to know "first and fast" if anyone has an issue with anything you say or do, it opens the channels for candid two-way communication so that you can avoid "spinach on your teeth syndrome." When leaders use the Velvet Hammer words, the conversation goes better for everyone involved, the person giving the feedback and the person receiving the feedback.

Another Velvet Hammer word that can be used effectively is "Really?" Really is an excellent conversation extender and listening tool when properly used. Your voice tone makes the difference here. When "Really?" is said empathetically or in a curious tone, it creates a rapport that encourages people to speak more. When used with jaded sarcasm, it has the reverse affect. Give "Really?" a try because "Really?" really works! Really!

Another Velvet Hammer word is "just." What I like about "just" is that it minimizes the point. There are a lot of theories about this word. One theory is to avoid using it because it devalues your actions, as in, "It's just me." Well, of course that's not a good use of the word. The better use is "We just need to discuss the situation a bit more thoroughly." It softens the communication, because "just" acts as a buffer or minimizer. Context is key.

At the end of a meeting you can say, "So just to summarize…," which indicates a brief review is about to happen in a nonthreatening way. You can also say, "So just to clarify, I'll do this, and you'll do that, and we will meet again next week." In this example "just" softens the action steps, making them more conversational and less of a command.

Another very effective way to begin a corrective "critical" conversation is to say "I need your help," because it's disarming. Here's an example using this Velvet Hammer phrase along with some of the others.

> **Corrective Feedback Formula:** "Got a minute? Great! Because I need your help. I noticed that you've been coming in late. (Pause) I was wondering what's causing this (pause), because it cannot continue. What do you suggest we do?"

The tone here is you are seeking to help rather than reprimanding. You set the expectation by saying "This cannot continue." Asking "What do you suggest we do?" makes the point that it's "us" (me and you) against the problem, instead of me versus you.

## Take Action!

1. Give the Velvet Hammer a try and see how it can work for you.

2. Insert "Noticed and Wondering" to start the conversation and "Likelihood and/or When" to end it. Apply the other Velvet Hammer words as needed.

3. Avoid "spinach on your teeth" syndrome by having critical conversations sooner rather than later by following the feedback "first and fast" expectation.

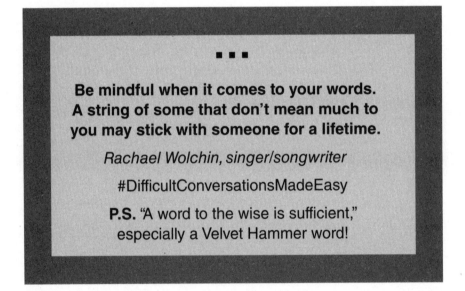

■ ■ ■

**Be mindful when it comes to your words. A string of some that don't mean much to you may stick with someone for a lifetime.**

*Rachael Wolchin, singer/songwriter*

#DifficultConversationsMadeEasy

**P.S.** "A word to the wise is sufficient," especially a Velvet Hammer word!

# 15

# THE LANGUAGE OF THE LANDS

**Q.** How do you communicate with someone you find impossible to relate to?

**A.** Answer: Learn the Language of the Lands.

Have you ever tried to speak with someone you could not relate to? You didn't really understand where the person was coming from. It was as if he or she were from a different country, world, or planet. Have you ever said to yourself, "I just don't understand this person" or "He is impossible to work with!"?

Well, you're not alone! It is true that people can be very difficult to understand, to relate to, and to work with. Of course, being flexible and adaptable definitely helps. Learning the Language of the Lands helps even more. You may be aware that there are four distinct personality types. Numerous personality profiles are fascinating, fun, and intriguing to take because they help us understand ourselves and others better.

They also help us realize that people are different more than difficult. Once you gain an understanding of the differences based on personality, this awareness will make it much easier to connect with, relate to, and work with others. Granted, some personalities are completely off-the-charts, out-of-the box, and practically impossible to deal with, but for the most part, people fit into one of four classic personality types: Social, Factual, Helpful, and Driven.

They go by various other similar names depending on what personality profile you are accustomed to. Each type has a hot button and a language unto itself that is spoken fluently, albeit unconsciously. Each type has a hot button that gets the person's attention, words that trigger an emotional connection or reaction.

Understanding the different personality types is valuable because they make you more aware of your own behavior and communication style and give you ways to successfully work with others.

Discovering the four different hot buttons and how to use them is priceless! This builds a bridge with people you may not naturally connect with and helps you to be more relatable, likeable, and trusted, three very important characteristics in relationship building and maintenance.

**Warning:** Be careful not to assume that because you have taken certain personality profiles you can think, "Been there, done that." This may cause you to miss important insights in this chapter. If you master the Language of the Land, you will have an advantage in the way you communicate with just about anyone.

**Note:** A great deal of the information in this chapter is based on personal experiences as well as on a study I did in my organization. I hired one of each of the four types so I could study them over a three-year period. Of course, I told them they were in a study on interpersonal communication and team dynamics, so there was full disclosure and transparency.

Below is a simple guide to help you communicate and connect with the four basic personality types. It consists of eight words that unlock the mystery of how to get along with just about anybody.

Social = AMAZING!    Driven = WIN

Helpful = HELPFUL    Factual = RIGHT

By knowing when to use the eight words, you can bring cohesiveness to even the most complicated relationships. You just need to know that there are four different types of people and each speaks the Language of the Land. Saying just one word in his or her language makes all the difference and begins building a bridge of cohesiveness.

**Example:** When I was in Greece, I knew no Greek. (It was all "Greek to me.") When I bought merchandise in the marketplace it was trans-actional with little to no emotion because I didn't speak the language. I asked someone who spoke English, "How do you say thank you in Greek?" The reply was "Efkharisto." After my next purchase, I said, "Efkharisto!" The reaction I received was an enthusiastic "Parakalo!" meaning you're welcome. It was fascinating how *one word* in the native language could so drastically change the interpersonal communica-tion. The words Amazing, Helpful, Right, and Win can have the same dramatic affect because each of these words fits in the native language of a personality type.

## THE HOT BUTTON OF THE SOCIAL TYPE IS TO BE AMAZING!

Their language is centered around the word *amazing*! They say it all the time, as in: "You're amazing! It's amazing! That's amazing! Isn't it amazing?" The second most common word Social types use is "great," and they use it all the time as well, as in, "That's great, it's great, you're great! Isn't it great!" If you are not from the Land of Social, you may wonder how everything can be so great. Do you know people who talk like this? Do you speak like this?

Social types don't just like to be amazing, they LIVE to be AMAZING! To be noticed and to stand out is essential to them. They also LOVE recognition. *They fear rejection, being excluded.*

Socials typically laugh at humor regarding the unexpected. To speak their language and connect with Social types, tell them that they are amazing or that what they've done is amazing—or great.

## THE HOT BUTTON OF THE FACTUAL TYPE IS TO BE RIGHT

The language of their land consists of words like, "You're right." Absolutely, exactly, and precisely are also frequently used. If you are not from the Land of Factual, you may wonder what the big deal is to make a mistake or get something wrong. It may not make much of a difference to you, but it makes a huge difference to them. Their language is centered around precision, so they are right more than any other type.

My husband is from the Land of Factual. He is a builder. Would you rather hire a Factual builder or a Social builder? I'd choose Factual. One day I walked into an addition that he was building and proceeded to tell him how "amazing" it was. He ignored me and walked away. I thought he had a negative attitude. I thought to myself, "How can I be married to a person who is so negative when I am so positive?" I was frustrated and disappointed, until I learned more about the types a few days later. The next time I went into the addition I said, "This addition is 'exactly' how I pictured it, the way the beams line up so 'perfectly.' Now I was speaking his language and his whole face lit up.

He looked so happy and engaged as he enthusiastically said, "Yes, and look over here. This beam is eye-level, but not level-level. Take a look. Here's the level." Actually, I didn't really care about the level. I would rather have him say that I was amazing! But he would never say that because Social-speak is a foreign language to him. Once I understood the magic of the Language of the Land, it literally saved our marriage.

The Factual don't just like to be right, they LIVE to be RIGHT. *Factuals most fear being wrong.* Factuals typically laugh at humor involving mistakes.

## THE HOT BUTTON OF THE HELPFUL TYPE IS TO BE HELPFUL

Their language is centered around helping others. One of my assistants, Eileen, is from the Land of Helpful. One day in the office she asked if I wanted some water. I said no thanks. She went on to ask if I would care for some tea. I was fine. When she offered to get me a tuna sandwich, I realized that I had to say yes to something or she was not going to stop asking. Do you know anyone like this? Are you like this? When I asked Eileen what her favorite compliment was, she said, "I couldn't have done it without you." To her that was the best because it meant she was so extraordinarily helpful!

Helpful types don't just like to be helpful, they LIVE to be HELPFUL. *They fear being helpless.* Helpfuls typically laugh at humor involving good intentions gone wrong.

## THE HOT BUTTON OF THE DRIVEN TYPE IS TO WIN

They are all about "on to the next." You're either a winner or a loser to them. Useful or useless. "Help me win or get out of my way" is their modus operandi. Their language is centered all around winning. They use phrases like "What's the point?" "How does that impact the bottom line?" So you better be good or be gone to work effectively with them.

I have an attorney who is the Driven type. We were closing on a house that had liens. The judge was taking way too long to sign off on them. The attorney said, "Don't worry, I'm bird-dogging the situation." A bird. A dog. A hunt. Classic Driven-speak. My husband asked what was going on with the closing. I said, "Don't worry, he's bird-dogging the situation. He said, "What?" Being from the Land of Factual he didn't speak Driven. A few days later we received another call from our attorney. He said, "I've applied enough pressure. They should be crumbling any day now." The bottom line is we got the house.

Driven types don't just like to win, they LIVE to WIN. *They fear incompetence of others.* Drivens typically laugh at humor involving absurdity.

## APPLYING THE FOUR TYPES

Here's a quick self-test. Ask yourself whether you would rather:

**A.** Be amazing

**B.** Be right

**C.** Be helpful or

**D.** Win

Sometimes it's easier to determine your type by deciding what you are not. Take the self-test again. This time ask yourself what you *don't* need to be.

You can also tell what type you and others are in the following four ways:

1. **Vocabulary.** People tend to use the vocabulary of their own type. By listening carefully, you can detect it in yourself and others.

2. **Occupation.** Many people tend to choose a profession that plays to their strengths and suits their personality type. Accountants tend to be Factual, sales reps tend to be Social, customer service reps tend to be Helpful, and attorneys tend to be Driven, for example. Of course, any type can be any profession if they are passionate, skilled, or smart enough to do something that is not as natural for them to do.

3. **Body Language/Facial Expressions.** Most Socials and Helpfuls are more demonstrative in their body language and facial expressions than the Factuals and Drivens are.

4. **Sounds.** Each type makes a specific sound. Listen for it:
   - Social's sound is a celebratory "Yay!" (as in "Whoohoo!")
   - Factual's sound is a reflective "Ahh" (as in, "I get it!")
   - Helpful's sound is a sincere "Aww!" (as in, "How nice.")
   - Driven's sound is an insightful "Hmmmph" (as in, "You've got my interest.")

When you or others make the same sounds, it means that you have made a deeper connection.

## THE CHAMELEON

If you are not sure of your word or sound preferences, you may be the Chameleon type. This type is so mild in the category that he or she can relate to any type easily. If you think you are a combination of two types, that is also possible. For instance, you can be a Social with Driven tendencies, or a Helpful with Factual tendencies because you border two types.

By hiring one of each type, I was able to study their language and work habits while they were working for me on a daily basis. During the study, I noticed that each personality type used words to communicate that the other types did not.

The next chapter provides valuable insights on how to actually learn to speak the language of each land.

---

## Take Action!

1. Embrace the concept that people are different more than difficult.

2. Notice the words others use when speaking. See if you can detect the land they are from.

3. See if you can begin to speak the Language of Lands other than your own country of origin with prospects, clients, staff and management.

■ ■ ■

**I don't like that man. I must get to know him better.**

*Abraham Lincoln*

*My updated interpretation of Lincoln's quote:*

**I don't like that person. I must not know him or her very well.**

#PeopleAreDifferentMoreThanDifficult
#BeAwareOfTheLanguageOfTheLands

**P.S.** We can all get along better by speaking each other's languages better.

# 16

# SPEAKING THE LANGUAGE OF THE LANDS

**Q.** How can you become fluent at speaking the Language of the Lands?

**A.** Practice, practice, practice.

From the extensive research I have done on personality types, I came to the conclusion that each type speaks a distinct language, just as people from different countries speak the language of their country of origin. If you were to imagine that those from the Land of Social speak Social, those from the Land of the Factual speak Factual, those from the Land of Helpful speak Helpful, and those from the Land of Driven speak Driven, it will help you to be multilingual and relate better to more people. More people will relate to you, too!

The ideal is to be like the Swiss. Natives of Switzerland are multilingual. Can you guess some of the languages you would speak if you were of Swiss origin? You would most likely speak four different languages: English, French, Italian, German, and Romansh because Switzerland borders many countries. To communicate more fluently and effortlessly with different types of people, being aware of the different languages they speak is a good first step.

The second step is to start deliberately practicing words from other "Lands." Although awkward at first, like any new language is to acquire, the payoff is huge! Have you ever walked by people who were speaking Spanish? You knew they were speaking Spanish because you were familiar with the cadence and sound of the language. I walk by people who are speaking Social, Factual, Helpful, and Driven and can tell their country of origin. For instance, the other day I walked by two businessmen. I heard one say, "You know you're right about that." The other said, "I'm not exactly right." It was obvious to me that they were both from the Land of Factual.

To become more fluent with the different types' languages, practice on non-important conversations. When I first started to listen for key words that clued me in to other personalities and attempted to speak the language, I did it with taxi drivers in New York City. If I made a mistake, it didn't really matter. I would also practice in restaurants. I would size up my waiter and attempt to speak his language. Be careful when beginning this initiative. You can and most likely will make mistakes.

The first time I tried to speak the language of one of my clients it was quite awkward, so I recommend practicing on non-clients first. We were in his office and he offered to lend me some books. I thanked him and was about to leave when he asked, "Do you need a box to carry them in?" I said, "No, thanks. I'm fine." He looked at the number of books I had in my hands and said, "No, I think you need a box." I said, "OK."

As he was looking for a box, I started thinking ahead to what I was going to say when he put the books in the box. My native tongue being Social, normally I would say, "Great!" But now with this new insight to the Language of the Lands I wanted to speak his language, so I decided instead of saying, "Great!" I would say, "Perfect!" He returned with the box and put the books in them. As he was closing the box I noticed that the stack of books was slightly higher than the box. But I was ready with my Factual word. I said, "Perfect! Thank you."

He looked at the box being a bit too small and said, "Well, it isn't exactly perfect is it?" Then he went to see whether he had another box that would be a better fit. This amused me because I felt I now had a deeper understanding of how to communicate with him.

He was right! (Of course he was!) The box wasn't perfect. In my attempt to speak his language I disregarded that fact, which was a typical Social move. He was also right when he said that I needed a box, because the books would have slid all over the back seat of my car. They could have been damaged. That thought never crossed my mind. He returned with a slightly bigger box. I said, "Perfect!" thanked him, and left. This time it was the right word.

## IMPROVING YOUR COMMUNICATION SKILLS

Once you are aware of the four types and four hot buttons and start listening for and speaking the Language of the Lands, you will have a new appreciation for how to take your communication skills to a higher level by connecting with people in a more meaningful and important way.

In sales, what type of personality do you think a buyer would be? If you said Factual, you would be right. (You may not need to be right, but that is the correct answer.) Company heads are usually the Driven type because they plow their way to the top. The Helpful types tend to be the gatekeepers. Sometimes gatekeepers are Factual. Since most sales professionals are Social types, they tend not to naturally speak the language of those who make the decisions, or even those who provide access to the decision-makers. Being aware of the Language of the Lands can strengthen relationships and increase revenue and profitability in any organization.

Maintaining an awareness of the Language of the Lands can help you to become much more successful in your career and life.

## TRANSLATING COMPLIMENTS

*Note:* Being a Social type, I have learned to do what I call the "compliment translation" (like a Google translation). Now whenever my husband says that I am right, I tell myself that he meant I was AMAZING! When I do the compliment translation, I feel a surge of positive energy and happiness because words matter. They are containers of power. How are you using yours?

Once you become more aware of the Language of the Lands, you can give yourself the compliment you deserve when your manager, client, spouse, or friend misses the mark. The hot button words happen to resonate more. This is an important concept because behavior rewarded gets repeated. Because compliments are a verbal reward, it's critical that they be given and received/heard properly. The right compliment to the right type of person can have a tremendous impact on morale, motivation, productivity, teamwork, and profitability. It truly is that powerful.

*Example:* I once asked a Factual client who was the director of human resources at a major publishing company in New York City, "What's so bad about being amazing?" He said, "There is absolutely no tangibility to the word whatsoever." He went on to say, "If you said that I was amazing because I was able to manage the building expansion project on schedule and under budget, then I would take your 'amazing' compliment to heart, respect it, and appreciate it. But just to be told I am amazing and not to say for what is meaningless to me." Interesting.

One of the saddest examples of being unaware of the Language of the Lands happened when I was speaking at the American Management

Association. After I had explained the personality types, a young sales account rep came up to me at the break and said, "My father never gave me a compliment in his life. I asked what type his father was. He said he was a Factual. I asked what type he was and he replied, "Social."

I then asked whether his father ever told him he was right. He said, "Yes, all the time. We used to do woodworking projects together in the garage. We worked side-by-side quietly most of the time."

I said, "I hate to tell you at this late date, but your father was giving you compliments all along if he was saying you were right and precise. You just couldn't hear them because he wasn't speaking your language." This was sad because his father was no longer alive. But by discovering the Language of the Land, he was able to at least know that he did receive compliments and was appreciated by his father.

One client of mine was from the Land of Driven. She said people from her land don't need compliments. "How can that be?" I asked.

She said, "We tell ourselves on a daily basis how we are doing. The input of others is not required. We actually get suspicious when complimented because we use compliments as a tactic to butter people up." I told her she would be better off if she complimented her team members. At first, she couldn't use any compliments without sarcasm. But then she discovered she could say "Super!" or "Excellent!" with sincerity and enthusiasm. Sometimes you have to "Salt the Hay" (Chapter 3) to find a way to be able to say the right words.

A Factual manager that I worked with said he had a hard time speaking the language of other types. I told him he could gesture a thumbs up. He tried it. It worked! This is because when the various types receive a positive sign like a thumbs up, they tell themselves the positive words they like to hear. The Socials interpret it as amazing, Helpfuls interpret it as being helpful, Factuals interpret it as being right, and Drivens rarely need a compliment, but they tell themselves they are on track, which is a win for them.

## Take Action!

1. Listen for the specific words people use most often when speaking.

2. Notice the words you use most often when speaking.

3. Observe the compliments you and others respond to most. See whether you can give an appropriate compliment to someone who is from a different land than yours.

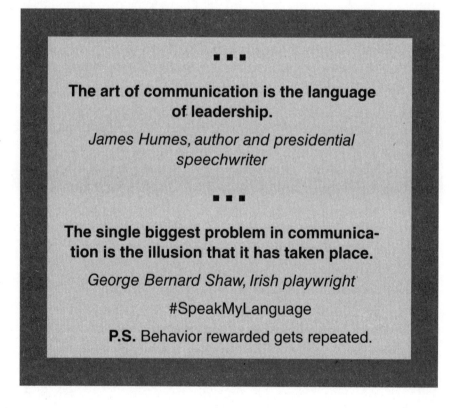

■ ■ ■

**The art of communication is the language of leadership.**

*James Humes, author and presidential speechwriter*

■ ■ ■

**The single biggest problem in communication is the illusion that it has taken place.**

*George Bernard Shaw, Irish playwright*

#SpeakMyLanguage

**P.S.** Behavior rewarded gets repeated.

# 17

# LISTENING=
# INTEGRITY

**Q.** Would you like to be a better listener?

**A.** Read on.

To become more fluent at speaking the Language of the Land of the people you will encounter, it is essential to pay careful attention to their word choices through active listening.

According to listening experts, you can count on one hand the number of very skilled listeners you will meet in your lifetime. The benefits of being a good listener are huge. Good listeners are better leaders, better sales professionals, better associates, and better at understanding and relating to others. Effective listening can have a direct impact on the success of your organization.

Being a good listener requires tremendous focus, attention, and effort, because most people think at over a thousand words per minute, but typically speak at about 125 to 150 words per minute, with gusts up to 175 wpm if speaking quickly. Because there is a time disconnect between thinking and speaking, it is easy to get distracted and not pay attention.

If you want to commit to be a better listener, applying the ideas in this chapter can help! Let's start by defining listening. The word "listen" comes from two Anglo-Saxon words meaning: to hear and to wait in suspense.

Listening is:

1. Receiving a message that's sent and understanding the meaning of the content and intent;
2. Sensing, interpreting, evaluating, and responding to the message;
3. Actively attending to the message, which requires high energy, genuine interest, and positive body language;
4. A gift you give yourself and others.

Now let's see how good a listener you are. Answer Yes or No to the following 15 questions. You may want to answer "sometimes" or "maybe," but do your best to answer Yes or No. If you really must answer in a different way, just give yourself half a point.

**Listening Quiz**

1. Do you talk more than you listen?　　　　　　　Yes　　No
2. Do slow speakers cause your mind to wander?　　Yes　　No

3. Does nervousness or fear sometimes prevent you from concentrating on a speaker's message?                Yes     No

4. When you are puzzled, annoyed, or confused, are you hesitant about asking questions?                Yes     No

5. Do you judge or criticize while someone is speaking?
   Yes     No

6. Do you frequently find yourself thinking ahead about something you want to say, even though the other person is still talking?
   Yes     No

7. When a problem comes up, do you often react without gathering all the facts, perhaps, by interrupting?                Yes     No

8. Do distractions, such as external noises or internal thoughts, prevent you from listening carefully?                Yes     No

9. Do you ever pretend you are listening, when you are really not?
   Yes     No

10. Are you very quick to give advice or offer a strong opinion?
    Yes     No

11. Do you believe that it is the speaker's responsibility to communicate effectively, as opposed to the listener's responsibility to listen actively?                Yes     No

12. Do you often think that you have heard someone's name, or an important fact, only to discover that you have forgotten it?
    Yes     No

13. Do you think listening involves only the ears and hearing?
    Yes     No

14. Do you think only about yourself and ignore the other person's feelings when you talk?                Yes     No

15. Do you think you were born with the ability to listen?
    Yes     No

If you answered "Yes" to any of these questions, your listening skills could be improved. If you answered "Yes" to more than five, you need to increase your ability to listen. Count your answers and see how you did. Did you get fewer than five? Congratulations. You are in a rare group of people who are very good listeners. Here is the answer key:

| | |
|---|---|
| 0 to 5 Yeses | Excellent Listener |
| 6 to 8 Yeses | Fair to Good Listener |
| 9 to 10 Yeses | Fair to Poor Listener |
| 11 to 15 Yeses | Poor Listener |

If you did not score well, it may help to know that most people do not score well on the Listening Quiz. The reason is that most don't realize that listening is a skill; like sports or music, it takes practice, time, and attention to become good at it.

The best way to improve your listening skills is to look back over the questions. Pick a question or two that you would like to change from a Yes to a No. When I did this, I chose to work on Question 7. I found that I was interrupting people too much, mainly because I was excited, more so than when a problem arose. Which questions do you struggle with?

The key to making positive change is to replace an old habit with a new habit. In the case of interrupting, I decided to replace the old habit of interrupting with the new habit of gently biting my tongue because I remember someone once saying, "You can tell the sign of a good marriage by the number of bite marks on the tongues of the people in the marriage. I took it literally. I figured out how I could gently bite my tongue without looking peculiar, and it worked! Below is a list of Ten Proven Ways to Be a Better Listener and Minimize Interrupting People. Bite Your Tongue is number 3.

**Ten Proven Ways to Be a Better Listener and Minimize Interrupting People**

1. **100% Responsible.** Each person in the communication dyad is responsible for 100% of the communication. It is not 50–50. It takes work to be a great listener. You have to be all in.

2. **Mirror Method and Check.** Repeat back what the person is saying. A good Velvet Hammer phrase to use when doing this is to say:

    "*So, just to clarify*, you are looking for XYZ; is that right?"

    You can do the silent Mirror Method when trying not to think ahead, as mentioned in Question 6. You can repeat silently to yourself what the person is saying, to stay with the person's thought process before jumping to conclusions and your own solutions.

3. **Bite Your Tongue.** You can literally (gently) bite your tongue to remind yourself to be more patient and physically prevent yourself from interrupting people. Try it. Now look in the mirror. Can you tell? You may have to try this a few different ways to get the most discrete positioning. It helps to practice by turning to someone to see if he or she can tell what you're doing. I've made a lot more money as a sales professional by biting my tongue versus talking. You can do it too. This technique can also help with Questions 2 and 7 on the Listening Quiz. Remember that you must replace an old habit with a new one to achieve successful behavior change. It's very difficult to just decide to talk less or to stop interrupting people.

4. **Drink Heavily!** This means water, tea, or coffee. You can *take a sip* when you ask questions. Better yet, you can choreograph your sips around the questions you ask. You can say, for example, as a manager: "How do you feel things are going on the project?" Then take a sip. Or, as an account executive: "What is the range of the budget you are targeting?" Then take a sip. Or as an accountant: "How did you come up with these numbers?" Then take a sip! Because you can't sip and talk at the same time, this technique works very well.

5. **Cover.** You can cover your mouth, especially when on the phone, to stop yourself from impulsively talking.

6. **Jot-a-Thought.** This works well because when you take notes you don't have to be concerned about forgetting your own ideas or the speaker's. Instead of saying, "I don't mean to interrupt, but…,: just jot your thoughts down and refer to them after the other person has stopped talking.

7. **4–4–6.** The 4–4–6 deep breathing exercise (described in Chapter 7) helps tremendously with listening effectiveness because it puts you in the present, where you have fewer distractions and are better able to focus on the message.

8. **Toe Press.** This involves pressing your toes into the ground. The toe press grounds you and provides a place for your energy to go.

You can do this seated or standing. It helps you stay present and focused on what others are saying.

9. **Purple Break.** A Purple Break (See Chapter 1) was invented by my father to stay energized. By covering and resting your eyes before an important meeting and restoring your visual purple, you will be more alert and able to concentrate better and longer in the meeting, making listening more effortless.

10. **The Five Times Rule.** This rule helps with Question 12 if you find yourself forgetting important facts or names. The trick is to repeat something five times (to yourself) and it's yours. Make an association. For instance, if you are trying to remember the name Jack O'Neil. You can associate it with Shaq O'Neal. My neighbor's dog's name is Brady, so I have used the association with Tom Brady to retain the name.

Listening is one of the most important skills you can possess. On any list of characteristics of great leaders, it is always one of the most essential. Listening takes time, effort, and practice to perfect, but it's worth it!

---

## Take Action!

1. Look at any "yes" answers on the Listening Quiz you took.

2. Make a commitment to change one "yes" to a "no" by applying the techniques listed above.

3. Make a commitment to consciously practice ways to be a better listener by attending to the message of the sender. The 4–4–6 and Toe Press are very effective here.

■ ■ ■

**One of the sincerest forms of respect is actually listening to what another has to say.**

*Bryant H. McGill, human potential thought leader, author, activist, and social entrepreneur*

■ ■ ■

**Most people do not listen with the intent to understand. They listen with the intent to reply.**

*Stephen R. Covey, American educator, businessman, keynote speaker, and author of The 7 Habits of Highly Effective People and other bestselling business books*

■ ■ ■

**Wisdom is the reward you get for a lifetime of listening when you'd have preferred to talk.**

*Doug Larson, columnist and editor for the Green Bay Press-Gazette*

■ ■ ■

**Be sure to taste your words before you spit them out.**

*Auliq Ice, singer, songwriter, rapper*

(Continued)

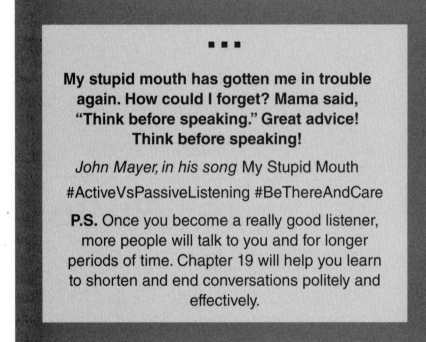

■ ■ ■

**My stupid mouth has gotten me in trouble again. How could I forget? Mama said, "Think before speaking." Great advice! Think before speaking!**

*John Mayer, in his song* My Stupid Mouth

#ActiveVsPassiveListening #BeThereAndCare

**P.S.** Once you become a really good listener, more people will talk to you and for longer periods of time. Chapter 19 will help you learn to shorten and end conversations politely and effectively.

# 18

# THE PLUS, PLUS, DASH

**Q.** Have you ever been stuck in conversations from which you could not escape? What to do?

**A.** Use the Plus, Plus, Dash.

Imagine yourself speaking on the phone or with someone at work or in a social setting, and you start to feel trapped. Your mind starts racing through the various ways to get out of this conversation politely and quickly without much luck. Has this ever happened to you?

It happens to most. The Plus, Plus, Dash can help! The Plus, Plus, Dash is a communication technique that can save you three to five hours a week. I created it based on a conversation with my best friend Mary. It has been field-tested and proven to work for the past 20 years.

Here's how it began: One afternoon I called Mary and asked if she was free to talk. She was at work and said: "Hi, Joy, I'm so glad you called, and I really want to talk to you. Right now, I'm under a tight deadline. When can we reconnect?"

I said, "Can you call me back in an hour?"

She said, "Yes!"

When I hung up I thought, "I'm not speaking with Mary, which was the purpose of my call. But I feel good. What did she just do?" As I traced back the elements of the conversation in my mind, I realized that she had made two positive comments and then she dashed off. From this encounter the Plus, Plus, Dash concept was created.

The next day I was delivering a time management seminar in New York City for the circulation department of a major magazine. I mentioned that I had a new technique that would save them time when conversations ran long or when they were interrupted and needed an out. I called it the Plus, Plus, Dash.

Here's how it works: When someone calls who is not a priority, and you have to stay on task, you can say, "I'm so glad you called (first plus), I really want to talk to you (second plus). Right now, I'm under deadline (transition). When can we reconnect? (dash) Immediately after giving this example, the response from one of the team was "We can't do that."

"Why not?" I asked.

"Because we are *not* really glad they called, and we really *don't* want to talk with them" was his reply. Everyone laughed, including me.

Seemed like I had to Salt the Hay on this one! (See Chapter 3 for more insights to Salt the Hay, Find a Way.) I knew the strategy would work. I just had to make a few adjustments. I asked the team: "Can you say 'thank you for calling' because you are a polite professional person?" They nodded yes. (Great! This is the first plus.) "Can you say, 'I want to talk to you,' because at some point you will have to since it's your job?" (This is a plus because it is inclusive.) They nodded yes. "Can you then say, 'Right now isn't the best timing. When can we reconnect?'" (the dash). They agreed they could say those things and realized the time savings as well as the benefits of the cordial approach.

Once I won over the tough publishing people, I discovered how a multitude of business people could benefit from the Plus, Plus, Dash and started getting feedback from many as to how much time it saves them.

Another Plus, Plus, Dash can go like this: "I saw you on the caller ID and picked up because I wanted to take your call. I wish I could talk now, unfortunately I am in the middle of something. When is a good time to reconnect?" The Plus, Plus, Dash is a way to handle interruptions and quickly go back to what you need to accomplish without missing a beat.

Initially, it's helpful to write down the Plus, Plus, Dash wording that will work best for you. If you are starting to think this seems scripted, you are right. I prefer to call it *rehearsed spontaneity* (for more on rehearsed spontaneity see Chapter 21, Presentation Is EVERYTHING!). It is about being planned, not canned.

The Plus, Plus, Dash provides a formula to divert interruptions to times when you can afford to have them. If an interruption occurs at a time that is more inconvenient than any other time, then it is best to go ahead and handle it with this formula.

Keep in mind that using the Plus, Plus, Dash method you become more in control of how your time is spent. Also, sometimes when you divert to a later time to speak, the person who called may find other ways to find answers and may not need you.

**Warning:** When using the Plus, Plus, Dash, be careful to avoid saying the word "but" as in "I'm glad you called, and I'd like to help *but....*" Because the word *but* acts as an eraser. It erases all the nice positive phrases you've used and emphasizes the dash. Some ask, "What can I use instead of *but?" However,* perhaps? Well, *however* has been described as a *but* in a tuxedo, meaning it is a more formal way of saying but.

The transitional phrase that seems to work best is "right now" (that is, "Right now I'm in a meeting. Can we talk at 4:00 p.m.?").

The Plus, Plus, Dash is a time management tool that will help you feel more in control of interruptions. It allows you more often than not to defer them to a more convenient time when you are less harried and have better focus, as opposed to dealing with everything as it comes up. Once you have perfected this technique, you will feel more confident in the way you handle interruptions and take charge of how you handle your time.

One client said, "To save more time we call the Plus, Plus, Dash, PPD. We use it in the subject of internal emails to say we're busy. It has saved us hours of time."

When Will Hart, who has worked with me for years as my reverse mentor (see Chapter 19 for more on Will), went off to college, I called him one night to see how he was doing. He answered his cell phone, said, "PPD 8" and quickly hung up. I was surprised by this, thought a few moments, and then wondered whether he meant Plus, Plus, Dash, I'll call you at 8:00. Sure enough, my cell phone rang at 8:00 p.m. and the corporate culture code was born. I asked him what he was doing when I called. He said he was having dinner with some new friends from the dorm. He wanted to answer but couldn't talk, so he thought I would figure out the code.

I thought that was genius. This time-saving code can also be texted or put in the email subject line. Curious, I asked, "What did your friends at dinner think when you did that?" He laughed and said, "They all wanted to know what PPD 8 was." He was at Emerson College having dinner with some of the brightest tech minds, all eager to know what PPD 8 was, and they loved it!

**Warning:** You can't *always* use the Plus, Plus, Dash. Sometimes you must take the call. When you take the call, you can still *ease into* the Plus, Plus, Dash after 5 to 10 minutes by saying, "I'm glad we had a chance to speak (plus). Thanks for going over the next steps (plus). I'll get right on it (dash).

## Take Action!

1. Write out the best wording for your Plus, Plus, Dash Plan to make it natural and yours.

2. Share the PPD culture code with others to save time and minimize interruptions.

3. If you must take a call or stay involved in a conversation, use the PPD to minimize it.

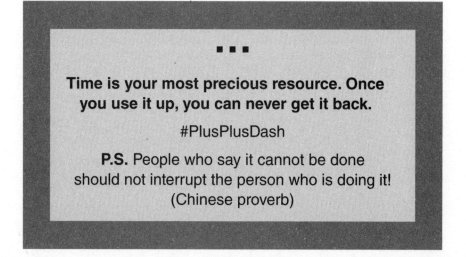

■ ■ ■

**Time is your most precious resource. Once you use it up, you can never get it back.**

#PlusPlusDash

**P.S.** People who say it cannot be done
should not interrupt the person who is doing it!
(Chinese proverb)

# 19

# THE WORDS
# MATTER
# MOVEMENT

 Do certain words motivate you more than others?

Yes!

The Words Matter Movement involves being a practitioner of careful, thoughtful, and deliberate positive communication. It is so easy to speak without thinking—to not genuinely listen and connect with people. When words are used in the wrong way, it can be devastating for the listener.

Words motivate or deflate thoughts hopes, dreams, and actions. Words have the power to excite, inspire, elate, sadden, frighten, anger, or give hope. Language is behavior. What you say matters. It shapes your environment, your work, and your life.

I am particularly aware of the power of word use because my father would refuse to hear negative words. He literally would say, "I can't hear you" when I would whine or complain about something when I was a young child. I naturally would say the same annoying whine, only louder. It wasn't until he said, "I can't hear you; I only can hear positive words" that I realized I was going to get what I wanted only if I asked in a more positive way.

Unbeknownst to me at the time, he was treating the way he communicated with me like a behavioral science experiment. My dad, having an extensive psychology background, was practicing the B.F. Skinner approach to behavioral psychology in shaping my communication style. The good news is that it worked! It conditioned me to look for the positive and speak from a more positive thought process with my staff and clients, and ultimately raise my children in a positive way.

Being acutely aware of the importance of word choice and language when communicating, one day I was driving my son Wilson home from school when there came a 'teachable moment' for us both about word choice. Wilson was seven years old. He was in the back seat of the car, propped up in his car seat. I started telling him about all the things he was going to be doing that afternoon. I said, "Wilson, we have to get you a haircut, and then we are going to Cooper's house for a play date, and then you have a lot of homework to do."

I could see by looking at him in the rearview mirror that he was clearly not happy about this. He said, "Mom, it's too much!" And then he said in a very angry and emphatic tone, "What are you … nuts?!"

I was stunned. I had never heard him speak like this before. He had never been so blunt and rude. Immediately, I said, "Wilson! Watch your words. We don't talk like this in our family. That was not a nice thing to say. Don't ever speak to me like that again." I was so upset.

Wilson, being quick-witted, rephrased his comment with a smile. Without missing a beat, he said, "OK, then, what are you … cashews?!" At which point we both burst out laughing.

I said, "That's genius!" and I rearranged his afternoon plans and added more downtime for him. Would you rather be called nuts or cashews? Cashews works better for me.

It reminds me of when I was in the office with my "reverse mentor" Will Hart. Will started working for me when he was 12 years old because he was a computer wizard with an abundance of technical talent. Although he was mature for his age, one day when he was about 15 I said something that I thought was very funny. Will looked at me like I was crazy and said, "You're so weird." I didn't want to be weird, I wanted to be funny! His words contained power because they bothered me.

A few days later, it happened again! I said something I thought was funny, and he said, "You're so weird!" the word "so" made it worse.

I had to tell him how I felt. I said, "Will, when you say I am weird when I am trying to be funny, it hurts my feelings."

He said, "But you are weird when you think you're funny."

I said, "Well then, regardless, the next time I am trying to be funny and you think I'm being weird, can you please say, 'You're funny or you are so funny!'?" He agreed. Since I like to see the humor in things, it didn't take long for me to see the humor in something and say it.

At this point Will said, "You are soooo funny!"

"Really?" I replied. "Do you mean funny, funny or weird funny?" He said, "Weird funny." I was OK with that because it took the sting out of it.

Another time a few weeks later I said something I thought was hysterical when working with Will. He started to laugh and said, 'That's funny!" I said, "Do you mean it was funny, funny or weird funny?"

He said, "No, that was hysterical!" And of course, that made me feel great because of the validation.

When he would say I was being "funny" (meaning weird) it didn't bother me, because I knew I was funny, even though he still meant I was being weird. In a strange way, I could handle being called weird better when it was disguised in the word funny. When I spoke about this wordplay in a keynote presentation on leadership and the important role of effective communication, someone came up to me afterward and thanked me. She said she realized that one of her associates was always saying that she was a perfectionist, and it was increasingly bothering her. She said by listening to the stories I told, she now knew how to handle it.

Your environment shapes you. Words are a significant part of your environment. If you want positive change in your work and life, watch the words around you.

One last example is from a time when I was a child and we entered our guinea pigs in a pet competition at the Nature Center. As the judges were walking around looking at the kittens, parakeets, and puppies, it was hard to imagine how they could make their decision. I mentioned this to my dad, who immediately took a pen and paper out of his pocket and wrote something on it and put it on top of the cage just as the judges were walking by.

They looked at the cage and the note, smiled, and went to have a quick chat. Then one of the judges announced into the microphone: "The winner of this year's pet competition is the Baldridge family and their guinea pigs Matilda and Lucky, who are here on their honeymoon!" "On their honeymoon" was the differentiator. Three simple words. Words are containers of power. Words *matter*. How are you using yours?

## Take Action!

1. Become aware of the words you use in daily conversations. Do they tend to be more positive or negative?
2. Notice what words motivate you and those with whom you interact.
3. Challenge yourself to think about positive word choices and how to up your game.

■ ■ ■

**Your words become your world.**

*Nadeem Kazi, world-renowned for peak performance, motivation, and his self-excellence academy*

#WatchYourWords

**P.S.** You can change the course of your life with your words.

## Words Are Containers of Power!

On a business flight from Dubai, UAE, to Amman, Jordan, I was reading *Rolling Stone* magazine when I discovered powerful words that resonated with me, that I feel compelled to share with you. They were in a Q & A piece featuring John Mayer, reported by Patrick Boyle.

While in Dubai, I conducted a seminar entitled, "The New Rules of Leadership." I emphasized the concept of "Words Are Containers of Power."

While reading the *Rolling Stone* article, I was struck by the power behind the words John Mayer used when answering Doyle's questions. When asked about some "low shots" Chris Robinson, formally of the Black Crowes, said about Mayer on *The Howard Stern Show*, Mayer replied, "I care about this band too much to give that life." I thought this was a brilliant use of words!

He went on to say, "I'm done debating my own merits. No, I know I am very good!"

Imagine taking on Mayer's words and owning them the next time you feel down or experience criticism. To refuse to "give life" to it and instead validate your self-worth. Having these words at the ready is a good way to go—to be done debating your own merit and proclaim that you are very good.

He went on to say, "For all the moves I've made on the musical chessboard, I am now me." I love the imagery of those words. Don't you? Have you made enough moves on your life's chessboard to be you? If words are containers of power, how are you using yours to influence the next move on your chessboard? Do you "care too much" about yourself and your reason for being to "give life" to any negative thoughts or experiences? Yes or no?

After all the moves on your life's chessboard, are you now you? *Moral:* "Give life" to the good and enjoy being you!

Reference: *Rolling Stone*, July 2017, page 30

# 20

# THE HAPPINESS ALPHABET

**Q.** How do you put yourself in a better mood when you're in a bad mood?

**A.** Recite the Happiness Alphabet.

The Happiness Alphabet is an activity I used to do with my mom when she was not feeling well. She was usually a very positive, productive, practical, and successful businesswoman. A real problem-solver. But there were a few rare times when her thoughts would turn negative during her cancer treatments, making life tough. To get through those tough times, she would write down the letters of the alphabet and put a positive word next to each. When I would visit her, we would say them out loud. She, or I, would say a letter, and then we would each say a positive word beginning with that letter, and it would elevate our moods. Below is an example of one round of the Happiness Alphabet.

A is for Awesome

B is for Beautiful

C is for Creative

D is for Delightful

E is for Enthusiastic

F is for Fantastic

G is for Gorgeous

H is for Hilarious

I is for Incredible

J is for Joy

K is for Kind

L is for Love

M is for Marvelous

N is for Nice

O is for Outstanding

P is for Prosperous

Q is for a Quiet

R is for Resilient

S is for Sensational

T is for Terrific

U is for Unbelievable

V is for Vivacious

W is for Wonderful

X is for X-Factor *

Y is for Youthful

Z is for Zealous.

For the cynics reading this saying, "Oh pleeeze. ..." What if we were to do the Anti-Happiness Alphabet? Perhaps that might make you happier.

If so, it might look something like this:

A is for Awful, B is for Brutal, C is for Catastrophe, D is for Disaster, E is for Errors, F is for Failure, G is for Gross, H is for Horrendous, I is for Idiot, J is for Jerk, K is for Kaput, L is for Loser, M is for Miserable, N is for Never (as in, "Never going to happen!"), O is for Obnoxious, P is for Peon, Q is for Quitter, R is for Ridicule, S is for Stupid, T is for Terrible, U is for Unnerving, V is for Vicious, W is for Worthless, X is for Xanthippe, Y is for Yo Mama or Yuck (sorry, that's the best I could do for Y), and Z is for Zero.

If the negative words make you happier than the positive ones, go for it! Whatever makes you happy works for me. Reading them makes me laugh because it is so absurd to have so many dreadfully negative words all in one place. The bottom line is that you become what you say to yourself, so choose your words wisely.

---

* X is always the hardest letter to find a positive word for. X-factor is a noun defined as a hard-to-describe influencer of quality. This word originated in 1934, not on the TV show with Simon Cowell. Online is a website named positivewordsdictionary. com. It lists several positive X words and, of course, other words too, in case you get stuck.

## Take Action!

1. Give it a try. Alone or with others, say each letter of the alphabet with a positive word after it.

2. You can actually write the Happiness Alphabet in different variations and review it from time to time.

3. Get creative! Come up with different positive words each time.

■ ■ ■

**Positive thinking is more than just a tagline. It changes the way we behave. And I firmly believe that when I am positive, it not only makes me better, but it also makes those around me better.**

*Harvey Mackay, successful businessman, columnist, author of* Swim with the Sharks Without Being Eaten Alive *and many other bestselling books*

Words are containers of power. How are you using yours?

#LanguageIsBehaviorBehaviorIsLanguage

**P.S.** Watch your words, because words matter!

# 21

# PRESENTATION IS EVERYTHING!

**Q.** What's the definition of a good presentation?

**A.** A good beginning, a good ending, preferably close together.

Presentation *is* everything. So how are you presenting yourself? What is the first impression that you make, and what is the last impression? How do you start a meeting, transition from point to point, and end a meeting? Franklin Delano Roosevelt once said when speaking about meeting success: "Be brief, be genuine, and be gone!" Rarely do people complain about a meeting running too short. It's when they go on and on that they become problematic. That's why you should bring your P.A.L. to every meeting, every meeting you run, and every presentation you give.

P.A.L. stands for Purpose, Agenda, and Limit! Your purpose is why you are speaking, the agenda is what you will be covering, and the limit is the time limit, how long you plan on speaking. Once you have your P.A.L. determined, you can focus on the content, organization, and style of your presentation.

- **Content:** What you want to say, facts, data, research, human interest stories, information, etc.
- **Organization:** What is the best order to have the greatest meaning and impact? Three is a magic number.
- **Style:** Word choice, voice tone, mood, manner, gestures, etc.

## THE 30-SECOND RULE

The best presentations begin and end by applying the 30-Second Rule. This rule involves writing out the first 30 seconds and the last 30 seconds of your presentation. Take time to perfect them. Focus on word choice and how you want to start and end your presentation. Fortunately, most presentations are best when the opening and closing are similar, as in the classic textbook presentation formula of: Tell them what you're going to tell them, tell them, and tell them what you've told them.

Those who do not know about the 30-Second Rule usually get off to a shaky start and then get in their groove before hitting their stride. This approach is awkward at best. Like jazz music, when presenting your message, you want to "burn from the first note." By applying the 30-Second Rule you will start and end your presentations with more confidence, conviction, and engagement.

**Warning:** Once you have written your 30-second opening and 30-second closing, don't memorize it, because you will sound "canned." The goal is to be planned (prepared), not canned. The act of writing your thoughts down solidifies them naturally. And don't forget to breathe! (See Chapter 7, 4–4–6 Breathing.)

## REHEARSED SPONTANEITY

Rehearsed spontaneity is when you prepare to be spontaneous. Mark Twain once said that it took him about three months to come up with one good spontaneous quip. If you notice things that make you laugh or think are profound, make a note of them and use them later in your presentations. It's much harder to be humorous or eloquent in the moment.

To help with your rehearsed spontaneity efforts, here are some phrases you can use to begin and end your presentations.

## WORDS, PHRASES AND QUESTIONS TO POSITION YOUR PRESENTATION, ENGAGE YOUR AUDIENCE, AND CLEARLY GET YOUR MESSAGE ACROSS

The following words, phrases, and questions have been proven to help position your presentation to be more conversational and engaging. Keep this list handy to peruse and select the best phrases and questions based on the objectives of your presentations/meetings.

### CONVERSATIONAL OPENING PHRASES AND QUESTIONS

Before we get started… Who here has noticed…? I was wondering/curious….

You may be wondering/curious why/about….

While preparing for this meeting, I realized…. What struck me/I was struck by/I noticed/I was impressed by….

There are three core aspects to….

The purpose of this meeting is three-fold, to 1, 2, 3

I'm here to share/provide/go over/summarize/clarify

Typically, we… Routinely, we… Usually, we….

What is most important is… What you need to know first is…
What affects you is… and here's how…

There's a reason why…

Imagine if…

My recommendation/suggestion is…

I was struck by… It was fascinating how… Trends show…

## CHECK-IN QUESTIONS

Can you see how this will make a difference?

Does this make sense? How does that sound?

**Transitions:** So, and, now that, next, because, here's what's important…

## CLOSING PHRASES AND QUESTIONS

So, to summarize… So, to clarify…

The logical next steps are… (step is)

What makes the most sense to do is…

If you remember nothing else from this presentation, remember this…

## AVOID WEAK LANGUAGE

Try to… Hope to….

**Remember:** The key is to practice, review, and use these effective phrases and questions so you can position yourself to be *planned,*not canned. It is important to use the phrases and questions that you feel are most natural and effective. Keep the 30-Second Rule in mind. Plan the first 30 seconds and last 30 seconds of what you will say. Be sure to emphasize the value and variables of what your audience feels is most important to them and their goals. Make a list of the perceived value of your message to your audience. One of the best ways to provide value to your audience is to focus on what you want your audience to think, feel, and do as a direct result of your presentation.

## The Glitch Factor

Expect the glitch! There is almost always a glitch. Have you ever had a glitch when presenting? I was giving a presentation in New York City in a board room on Park Avenue to some top executives who had flown in from France. I was writing on a flip chart while facilitating a brainstorming meeting. I was writing lower and lower on the page, capturing all the ideas that were being shared. When I started to stand up straight again, I was pulled down. I couldn't understand what was happening until I realized my heel had gotten caught in my hem. To steady myself, I grabbed hold of the flip chart, but the stand was aluminum and couldn't hold my weight, so I started to fall. Next thing I knew I was on the floor, the flip chart on top of me. The attendees leaped up to help me. "Mon Dieu!" I heard a few exclaim ("My God!" in French). I was mortified! I doubt this will ever happen to you, but this story serves as a reminder that things can and will go wrong when presenting. Keep your cool. Breathe (use the 4–4–6 from Chapter 7) and you should make it through just fine.

Another presentation glitch occurred when I was ironing a skirt at 6:30 a.m. before an 8:00 a.m. presentation. The iron was so hot it burned a hole clear through the front of the skirt. I couldn't believe it! All I had was sweat pants as a back-up. The meeting was being held in a remote lake area in Minnesota. I was speaking to sales and management leaders on successful business strategies. I took the stage with confidence but could tell there were some curious looks from a few audience members. I stopped the presentation for a moment and said, "You're probably wondering why I am presenting to you in sweatpants." Then I held up the skirt I burned, looked through the hole and said, "Here's why." Everyone laughed and applauded. Sometimes it's best to speak about the proverbial elephant in the room, build trust, and move on.

## Overcoming Nervousness

Go to any presentation skills section in any bookstore and you will see titles like *Butterflies and Sweaty Palms* by Judy Apps, *I'd Rather Die Than Give a Speech* by Michael M. Klepper and Robert E. Gunther, or *I Can See You Naked: A Fearless Guide to Making Great Presentations* by Ron Hoff. Why? Because presenting is one of life's greatest fears for most people. Here are three ways to calm your fear:

1. **Understand it.** Why are you afraid? Understanding why helps you face it and deal with it. Some possible reasons are fear of forgetting, being asked a question you don't know how to answer, being judged, turning red, feeling or looking foolish.
2. **Breathe!** The 4–4–6 is very useful before and during a presentation.
3. **Toe Press.** Pressing your toes while presenting gives a good place for nervousness to go, because when you press your toes, nobody knows! It also grounds you.

## ANSWERING QUESTIONS

To handle questions effectively:

1. Allow enough time in your presentation for Q & A. Don't rush or go overtime.
2. Repeat the question by restating it in your answer.
3. Ask for clarity if the question is unclear to you.
4. If no one is asking questions and you would like to encourage them, pose the first question yourself. You can say, "One commonly asked question is…? Who has the next question? Say "Who has a question?" rather than "Does anyone have any questions?" This is more specific and gets a better response.
5. If you do not have the answer to a question, offer to check and email the information later.
6. When surprised by a question, you can say something like: "I will have to check on that." Or "To accurately answer that question, I will need to do some research and email you that information."

## WAYS TO ENGAGE YOUR AUDIENCE

Audience engagement is important to help them stay focused on your message and to create a positive learning experience. Use a combination of these techniques to keep your listeners engaged.

- Using analogies, stories, and anecdotes
- Putting the human touch in your presentation

- Incorporating ways to involve your audience
- Making eye contact
- Controlling the environment: seating, audio, lighting, temperature (SALT), screen, projector

---

### Take Action!

1. Write out your 30-second opening and 30-second closing.

2. Practice and rehearse until your opening and closing statements sound and feel natural.

3. Focus on the value of your message and not your nervousness when presenting.

■ ■ ■

**Effective speaking is a million-dollar skill, a pathway to success in all areas of your life.**

*Ty Boyd, executive communications and coaching business owner*

■ ■ ■

**If you think presentations cannot enchant people, then you've never seen a really good one.**

*Guy Kawasaki, American marketing specialist, bestselling author, and Silicon Valley venture capitalist*

■ ■ ■

**Simplicity is the ultimate sophistication.**

*Leonardo da Vinci, Italian inventor, painter, sculptor, architect, engineer, botanist, astronomer, and writer*

#BeBreifBeGenuineBeGone

**P.S.** Keep it simple!

# 22

# BECAUSE OF YOU

**Q.** • How do you recognize people who do great things?

**A.** • You present them with the Because of You award.

The Because of You award was created at a sales organization I used to work at years ago. I was always the number one sales producer out of about 100 employees. I won an incredible number of awards, tremendous trips, and company yacht adventures to exotic places. I looked forward to going to the monthly all-company meetings because I knew I would be recognized for my hard work. Being from the Land of Social, you can imagine how much I enjoyed the recognition! It was AMAZING!!

One day I was talking to an administrative assistant in the office. I asked whether she was going to the meeting that night. She said, "I don't really want to go." I asked why not. They were fun events with lots of great food and drinks, immediately following the award ceremony and company announcements. She said, "No offense, but the same people get recognized and a lot of other people work just as hard, but just because they don't make money for the company they don't get the recognition that they deserve." At that moment, the Because of You award was born.

The Because of You award is given because someone did something very nice, helpful, thoughtful, significant, or incredible for somebody else. Because of you, and all you do! Because of something special you did. Because of you, it was done. Because of you, I left happier on a tough day. Because of you, I was able to reach my goal. Because of you, work is a nice place to be. The recipient of the Because of You award has a picture taken with the award, which is typically a beautiful trophy. The winner keeps the award on his or her desk for two days to two weeks, then finds someone else who deserves it to present it to. If someone "makes your day," that's another opportunity to give the Because of You award away.

Keeping a visible listing of who receives the award and why is a great way to recognize people you work with. It is a morale booster, too. What have you done recently for somebody else that would be deserving of this award? You can give it to yourself as well!

You don't even need a trophy to do it. You can proclaim it right now! This reminds me of a time when my daughter Mackenzie was five and my son Wilson was 11. We were in the car and I was doing an extraordinary job of making their lives awesome. We went to the park, we went out for ice cream, we did homework, and we packed in a lot of great things in one afternoon. I decided I needed an award! So I proclaimed myself mother of the year. Because no one was calling, nominations were not coming in, but I thought I was doing something extra special, beyond the normal amount of creativity, energy, and great parenting.

I actually went to the local trophy shop and bought myself an enormous trophy and had "Mother of the Year" engraved on it. I would keep the trophy in the car and every once in a while, when I was exceeding the children's expectations, I would start the ceremony. Mackenzie would pull the trophy out of the backseat and hand it to Wilson in the front seat. Wilson would start the ceremony music by humming a tune. We all laughed. It was good fun.

The point is that when you work really hard it's nice to be noticed. If you are the type who doesn't have a need to be noticed, it's nice to be appreciated. Give the Because of You award concept a try and see how it creates a more positive, productive, and profitable work environment. Remember: Behavior rewarded gets repeated.

A client heard about the Because of You award and liked the idea, so I made one for her. She has been incorporating it into her management meetings. It's working well!

---

## Take Action!

1. Who do you know who is deserving of the Because of You award?

2. Decide whether you want to embrace this concept.

3. Create and order online a Because of You award trophy and start paying it forward.

■ ■ ■

**Brains, like heart, go where they are appreciated.**

*Robert S. McNamara, former Secretary of Defense*

#BecauseOfYou #MotherOfTheYear

**P.S.** Who do you know who deserves to be appreciated? Can you let him or her know sooner rather than later?

## Reverse Mentor Gold!

I can't stress enough the importance of having a reverse mentor in your business life. (A reverse mentor is a mentor who is younger than you and can keep you current as new technology, music, culture, and innovative communications evolve over time.) Will Hart is mine, going 10 years strong. Working with him has kept me current with technology, patient as a leader, and humbled as a person.

Ten years ago, I vividly remember going to my friend Rachel's house, feeling numb in disbelief, as I went to pick up my son Wilson from a playdate. I explained to Rachel that I had just left my tech guy back at the office. As I was telling him I had to leave to pick up my son, he was crossing himself while trying to salvage my computer files, which were rapidly disappearing before our eyes. Some sort of virus had infiltrated my system. I said to Rachel, "I think I need more tech support. I'm so upset about the files being lost, I definitely need backup." (This was pre-iCloud.)

She said, "You should call Will Hart."

I said, "OK. Do you have his number?"

"No, but I have his mother's number right here."

Taken aback, I asked, "Why would I call the mother of a potential tech person?"

"Oh, because he's 12."

I exclaimed, "He's 12?"

"Yes. He's actually playing football in the backyard with Wilson and Matthew."

I looked out the kitchen window as she pointed him out to me. I asked why she thought I should work with him, considering that my client list is a who's who of the best organizations in the world. She said because he was very smart and great with computers. He had actually built a computer at camp that summer.

I was willing to give him a chance. After some negotiating with his mother, Julie, we came to a fair hourly rate and Will started working for me setting up my new computer, installing the antivirus software, and over the years building a new website, perfecting marketing materials, editing videos, and setting up and managing social media as it came into fruition. There was nothing this kid couldn't do! I proclaimed him: Will Hart Boy Genius! (WHBG)

Despite progressing through middle school, high school, and on to college, graduating with honors from Emerson College, and then on to his career in television unscripted series and specials at TNT/tbs Turner Broadcasting System, Inc. Will has always and will always be there for me, albeit on a very part-time basis, as we continue to grow the Baldridge brand and bring more joy to the business world.

One year quite some time ago, Will and I had a few disagreements. I asked him years later why he didn't leave. He said, "Because I was in too deep. I wanted to see what was going to happen next." I joke with him that I'm sure one day, when he has moved on to producing the Emmys or the Oscars, that he will probably not be able to still freelance with me, but I hope that day never comes, a time when we would ever part ways. So I'll continue to be happy in the now. Because now is perfect! (See Chapter 6.)

**Will Hart at 12**          **Will Hart at 22**

# 23

# MEDITATION

**Q.** What's the first word you think of when you think of meditation?
Peaceful? Calming? Boring?

**A.** Do it anyway.

A meditation practice done twice a day for 20 minutes each time can transcend your thoughts and transform your life. My friend Mark Riesenberg's meditation practice of choice is Transcendental Meditation (TM). He says it is a simple, easy, effortless mental technique.

Mark teaches meditation to business executives. His philosophy is that you meditate in the morning as preparation for dynamic, successful activity and in the early evening so you can better enjoy your evening. You meditate before you eat because it slows your metabolic rate 16 to 20 percent (the rate slows down 8 to 12 percent when you are asleep or dreaming), and when you eat your metabolic rate goes up for digestion. Meditating before you eat is a practical consideration. The 20 minutes twice a day is for maximum results.

Mark learned TM in December of 1970 and hasn't missed a day since. Why? He says, "Because it works! All the benefits you hear about meditation are real. The benefits come from the release of stress. It's the deep, profound rest you experience during meditation that releases stress by creating calm."

Mark has been a certified teacher of Transcendental Meditation since 1972 and has taught thousands of people to meditate. The results are accumulative. When you are dedicated to your daily practice you can expect:

**The Big Three**

1. More energy and more consistency throughout the day—more wakefulness.
2. The ability to handle stress more effectively. Things that used to drive you crazy still occur but now are *less gripping, intense, and lasting.*
3. A general sense of well-being and happiness.

There are many other benefits, but these are the top three to expect. Go to www.tm.org to find out more about meditation. The endorsements on the TM website include:

Transcendental Meditation is a simple, natural technique. This form of meditation allows your body to settle into a profound state of rest and relaxation and your mind to achieve a state of inner peace.

*The Mayo Clinic*

Perhaps the greatest benefit is that it is relatively quick to learn and easy to master. No waiting weeks or months of practice before you see results. TM cuts right to the chase—taking only days and, for some, minutes before one feels reprieve from their painful and overwhelming thoughts.

*Forbes magazine*

According to the TM website: *"The TM technique is an effortless technique for recharging your mind and body"*—and creating a brighter more positive state of mind.

Other meditation techniques include:

- Breathing techniques
- Chanting
- Concentration techniques
- Contemplation/prayer
- Mindfulness
- Progressive relaxation/guided meditation
- Visualization

With regular daily practice, all of these techniques lead to positive results. Mark practices and recommends TM because it is one of the simplest to do and the easiest to integrate into your life. The key is to find what works for you and use it.

A client of Mark's incorporates meditation into her business plan. When asked why, she said, "It has a positive and direct impact on the bottom line. Calm translates to currency."

**Warning:** Many who try meditation discontinue it because they aren't sure whether they are doing it right, they get bored, their thoughts start racing about all the things they have to do instead, or they get hungry. Many internal and external distractions can inter-fere with starting a meditation practice. Do it anyway. Start small and build. Even a few minutes of meditation is better than none at all. The benefits are invaluable: clarity of thought, peace of mind, and a new sense of calm and feeling of well-being that is priceless.

---

### Take Action!

1. Decide on a good time in the morning and early evening to meditate. Set an alarm to remind you, because it is easy to forget to do it.
2. Set the timer on your smart phone for 5, 10, 15, or 20 minutes. Select the amount of time that will work best for you to start, then increase as you continue your practice.
3. Sit quietly and peacefully. Feel the calm. When inevitable thoughts surface, gently acknowledge and release them. Let the thoughts pass by like a cloud. Breathe. Relax. Think peace. Feel peace. Be peace.

---

■ ■ ■

**Meditation means dissolving the invisible walls that unawareness has built.**

*Sadhguru, Indian yogi, mystic, and New York Times bestselling author*

*#PeaceOfMind #Ommmmm*

**P.S.** You can do this! Put down this book. Set your timer and go!

# 24

# Bankruptcy, Cancer, and Heart Attack

**Q.** Have you ever experienced challenging times?

**A.** Of course you have! Everyone has. What happens next is the key.

The worst of times.....

Steve Jobs was ousted from his company. Elon Musk topped that! Not only was he ousted as the CEO of his own company, but he was fired while on his honeymoon! Being that he was the founder of SpaceX, co-founder of Tesla, co-founder of X.com, which eventually became PayPal, and many other successful organizations, the advice here is that, if you are going to fail, fail like Elon Musk or Bill Gates, who before launching Microsoft was a Harvard dropout and co-owner of a failed business called Traf-O-Data. But driven by his passion he later built the world's largest software company.

The Queen of England, Elizabeth II, called her "rough patch" *annus horribilis* in a speech to Guildhall on November 24, 1992, marking the 40th anniversary of her accession. She also said, "1992 is not a year on which I should look back with undiluted pleasure." That's royal-speak for the worst year ever! Windsor Castle was burning, two of her children were divorcing amid torrid scandals, and a tell-all book on Princess Diana's tumultuous angst was released. What was to be a celebration became an "honest reflection." Even the Queen has hard times.

In 2007–2009 when the U.S. recession hit, the Dow plummeted from 14,164 to 6,594, a more than 50% drop. I couldn't bear to open my bank statements. Did you happen to experience any loss during this time? (Most did, but some didn't.) When I finally got the courage to open them, 70% of my life's savings were gone. I vividly remember coping by reading a passage from *The Power of Positive Thinking* by Norman Vincent Peale that said, *"I refuse to accept defeat."* I would say it over and over day after day when the steady flow of business started to subside.

In 2009–2010, one of my best friends and mentor, Mark Riesenberg, AKA: Mr. Meditation (see Chapter 23), had his own *annus horribilis*. That was the year that he was diagnosed with cancer, declared bankruptcy, the bank foreclosed on his house, and he had a heart attack. His heart medication caused a mild depression. It started with his doctors saying, "Don't worry, it may be nothing." I agree with the first part. Don't worry. (See Chapter 4 on Worry, Anxiety, and Fear.) But I have known far too many who have been told this and looked further into things only to discover that "nothing" was indeed something.) So when in doubt, check it out!

"Cancer, bankruptcy, and heart attack are three of the scariest words in the English language," Mark said. He went through all three at once, while dealing with diabetes, foreclosure, and depression.

In his book, *Brightening Your Life's Path*, he writes about this experience. His core approach to coping was to keep up his daily meditation practice. He said, "As bad as things were, they would be far worse without it." (As mentioned in Chapter 23, meditation makes difficult thoughts and circumstances less gripping, intense, and lasting.)

Mark's approach was to say the following again and again:

- I know what I have.
- I have decided what to do about it.
- I am doing it.
- I will be fine.

Thankfully, Mark made it through the cancer, bankruptcy, and heart attack with the philosophy that "No matter what happens to you in life, no matter what life unexpectedly brings your way, you can still wake up every morning with the joy of being alive. You can still wake up with a big smile on your face and the love of life in your heart." Mark did just that. Mark was very fortunate. By following the advice of skilled and knowledgeable medical and financial professionals, he was able to rebound successfully and has a thriving meditation and business coaching practice (and I still have my BFF).

**Warning:** All outcomes are not as positive as Mark's. Both of my parents passed away from cancer. It's how you decide to deal with your particular situation that is important here. Do hard times cause you to panic, become distraught and fearful, or cautiously optimistic, practical, and hopeful?

**The Bottom Line:** The most successful people push through devastating times. Remarkable survival instincts kick in, and devastation doesn't stand a chance.

## Take Action!

1. Accept the situation. The sooner you accept what is happening, the sooner you can regroup, deal with it properly, and move on from disbelief and shock mode to problem-solver and solution-seeker mode.

2. Do something! Ask yourself, "What's the best thing to do in this situation?" Then do it!

3. Stay positive, no matter what. There's an upside and a downside to everything. Stay up. Up is better than down.

■ ■ ■

**When you get into a tight place and everything goes against you till it seems you could not hold on a minute longer, never give up then, for that is just the place and time that the tide will turn.**

*Harriet Beecher Stowe*

■ ■ ■

**There are no problems in life. Only situations with an abundance of possible solutions.**

*Ken P. Baldridge, my dad*

#ThisTooShallPass
#ToughTimesNeverLastToughPeopleDo

**P.S.** Be ready for the outrageously unexpected.

# 25

# BEE STINGER OUT

**Q.** What do you do when you feel the sting of something that went wrong in your business or your life?

**A.** Take the bee stinger out.

I had a client who was upset about a miscommunication that we had, and I felt just awful. Has that ever happened to you? If you're like me, this probably happens rarely because you do everything you can to provide the best possible experience for your clients.

I went to my dad, my sage, and told him what had happened. He said that sometimes when things don't go the way we would like or expect, it's like getting stung by a bee. It hurts for quite some time. I said, "Yes, it still hurts, and it's been a few weeks."

He said, "You know when a bee stings you the stinger stays in and keeps the flow of venom going until you pull it out. So the sooner you find and pull out the bee stinger, the sooner the pain will subside and you will recover. It sounds to me like you need to pull the bee stinger out on this one."

I said, "That's easier said than done."

For the next several weeks I kept torturing myself for not being perfect. Have you ever done that? Wallowed in regret? I replayed the misunderstanding over and over in my mind. It was haunting me.

The client's name was Robert. Every week or two when dad would see me he would ask, "How's Robert?"

"Oh, Robert," I would moan. "I feel awful," I would say. (In retrospect, it actually wasn't even that big a deal. We still ended up working together.) I was so embarrassed. I misunderstood what he wanted and didn't do the job to his specifications.

About a month later, dad asked, "How's Robert?"

I said, "Robert who?"

He said, "Congratulations! The bee stinger is officially out!" We laughed. Indeed, it was. Dad said, "Next time try to pull it out sooner." I promised that I would.

Coincidentally, I actually was stung by a bee a short time later. I looked down and saw that the stinger was still in my hand. Immediately, I pulled out the stinger. It still hurt, but not nearly for as long.

Are you obsessing about something that happened differently than you had wished? Can you do something to change it? If so, do so. If not, pull out the bee stinger. The sooner you pull it out, the better you will feel and the more productive you will be.

## Take Action!

1. Prevent what problems you can by doing and being your very best at all times. Don't let up.

2. When things go wrong and you feel the sting of regret, do what you can to resolve the situation.

3. Pull the bee stinger out sooner rather than later. Let it go and move on.

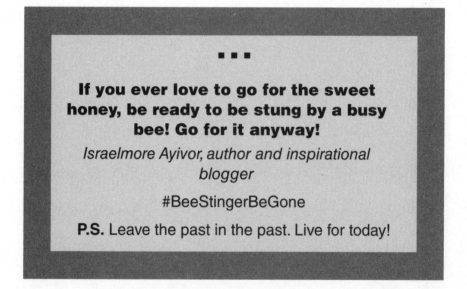

■ ■ ■

**If you ever love to go for the sweet honey, be ready to be stung by a busy bee! Go for it anyway!**

*Israelmore Ayivor, author and inspirational blogger*

#BeeStingerBeGone

**P.S.** Leave the past in the past. Live for today!

# 26

# What's Your "One Thing"?

**Q.** How can you be your very best?

**A.** Focus on the 'one thing'.

Now that Part 2 of this book is nearly finished, it would be a good idea to reflect on what you have read. Take a moment and flip back through the pages and note below the Golden Nuggets you would like to use before moving on to Part 3. Is it to use Velvet Hammer words, speak the Language of the Lands, listen better, apply the Plus, Plus, Dash, join the Words Matter movement? Have fun with the Happiness Alphabet, become a better presenter, give the Because of You award? Meditate, survive tough times, and/or take the Bee Stinger out? Once your list is complete, rank the top three things you will do differently, and commit to doing your "one thing" today.

**Favorite Golden Nuggets**

_____

_____

_____

_____

_____

My top three Golden Nuggets in order of importance:

1. _____

2. _____

3. _____

The "one thing" I will commit to do first is:

_____

_____

## Take Action!

1. Ask yourself each business day, "What's the one thing I can do to further my success for tomorrow?"

2. Do it!

3. Leave your day feeling satisfied!

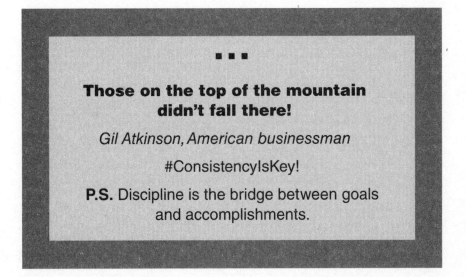

■ ■ ■

### Those on the top of the mountain didn't fall there!

*Gil Atkinson, American businessman*

#ConsistencyIsKey!

**P.S.** Discipline is the bridge between goals and accomplishments.

# PART 3

27

# ABDUCTION

**Q.** Have you ever had your thoughts abducted?

**A.** Here's how to get them back.

Some people's thoughts are abducted in the middle of the night, worrying about their workload for the next day. Some are abducted when things go wrong. Conditioning teaches us to think and feel certain things, due to circumstance either real or perceived. Have you ever had a visceral reaction to something that happened to you? You wanted to stay composed, but you had this sudden and pervasive feeling of dread, anxiety, or stress?

While I was on a run I saw an old white van slowing down. To most it would seem as if it was going to turn around or someone was going to ask for directions, but to me it caused an instant visceral reaction. It triggered a thought of when I was 11 years old and nearly abducted by a man in an old white van. Instantly, my thoughts turned to where to run if I needed to. As it turned out, the van simply drove away.

As I continued my run, I ran past a man who said, "The planes, the planes!" I stopped and asked, "The planes?"

He said, "There are too many planes flying above our town!" I was thinking what a beautiful day it was for a run, and he was fixated on the planes.

You never really know how someone is feeling or thinking, or what value the person places on what you do or say. It's hard to predict. You also never really know what you or others will think, feel, and do when interacting, especially when something startling, problematic, or unexpected happens.

This is where meditation (Chapter 23), deep breathing (Chapter 7), and removing the bee stinger (Chapter 25) help the most—when you are feeling the warning signs of danger. In these moments it's best to stop, take a moment, and take a breath to get back into the present.

So many things can and will try to abduct your thoughts, feelings, and actions each day. Being aware of this will calm you and lead to more clarity of thought and focused execution, when others might vent or freeze up. The next time you have a sale that is lost, an employee or co-worker who is difficult to deal with, or a personal situation that seems unbearable, keep them in perspective.

There is an old story of the snake and the rope. By the light of the moon a traveler thinks there's a snake in the road and is afraid. A villager says it is only a piece of rope. The snake the traveler imagined would bite him is really only a rope. Upon realizing this, the situation completely changes for the traveler. Once we perceive things as they really are, fear can be calmed and the situation dealt with rationally.

A director of a firm told me that he had a technique for keeping perspective and rationally tackling situations. When staff members would come to him with a problem, he would ask, "Is it a train wreck, or just burnt toast?" This worked most of the time to defuse a tense situation and deescalate stress. The only problem with this quick assessment was that some people he worked with didn't know the difference between a train wreck and burnt toast. These moments he turned into learning opportunities.

## Take Action!

1. When something bothers you, take a moment, take a breath, and put it in perspective.

2. Ask yourself "Is this as scary as I think it is?" If the answer is yes, write down the possible solutions and take action steps toward one of the solutions. If the answer is no, enjoy the sense of relief.

3. You will find once you reclaim your composure that your fear has less strength and power.

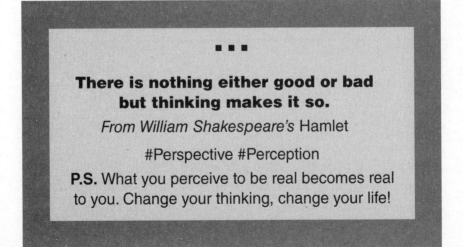

■ ■ ■

**There is nothing either good or bad but thinking makes it so.**
*From William Shakespeare's* Hamlet

#Perspective #Perception

**P.S.** What you perceive to be real becomes real to you. Change your thinking, change your life!

# 28

# LOST AND LONELY

**Q.** Ever get that lost and lonely feeling?

**A.** You're not alone.

The ROCK, aka Dwayne Johnson, actor and professional wrestler, said when speaking about his depression, "One of the most important things you could realize is that you are not alone. You're not the first to go through it. You're not going to be the last to go through it." He wished that he had someone at the time who could pull him aside and say, "Hey, it's gonna be OK. You'll be OK."

His depression began after being rejected by the NFL, while in his twenties. When things don't turn out as you plan, when you find yourself in a strange place in your life, chances are what you are experiencing has happened to many, many other people, despite how alone you may feel.

In college I was fortunate enough to be a part of the Semester at Sea program. Semester at Sea is sponsored by a university, as a fully accredited college program on a ship for one semester or about 100 days at sea as the ship sails around the world. The ship, aptly named the S.S. Universe, each semester has approximately 500 students from scores of different colleges and universities in the United States, 200 Taiwanese crew members, 50 faculty, and 50 adult passengers.

There are typically 10 ports of call per semester. On my voyage the 10 were Japan, Taiwan, Hong Kong, India, Sri Lanka, the Philippines, Indonesia, Egypt, Greece, and Spain. We left the United States in September from the Port of San Francisco and returned through the Port of Miami by December. It was the trip of a lifetime. One of the most fascinating places was India. Two friends of mine and I decided to go with our karma as we arrived at the train ticket office.

"Where would you like to go?" the clerk asked.

We said, "Wherever you want us to."

He was taken aback by that reply, so he asked us again, "Where would you like to go?"

We again said, "We are going with our karma, so where would you recommend? He printed out three train tickets to Coimbatore, which was 12 hours away from the station in Madras, now know as Chennai, where the ship had docked. We eagerly took the tickets and boarded the train. It was a rickety train and very crowded. We sat and talked. This was before smart phones. And we slept quite a bit. It was almost midnight when we got off the train. We were in a land that was very strange to us. Talk about a stranger in a strange land.

The roads were made of dirt and dust. Cows walking freely in the streets. Families were sleeping propped up against the closed storefronts. It was so dark. A man we befriended on the train happened to get off at the same stop. He asked whether we had a place to stay. We did not. He said, "I'll be right back." When he returned, he guided us to a door in the village. He knocked on it and a man inside said he would check to see whether there was a room available for us to spend the night.

At that moment I started to feel a little lost and lonely. I wondered, "What am I doing here? Going with my karma is not turning out to be quite as fun as I thought it would be." I didn't let on to my friends my concerns. They seem to be OK. While we waited to hear back from the man inside a small door on the dirt road, I looked around again and wondered about the people and families sleeping in each other's arms on the sidewalk. Then, for some reason I looked up and saw a strangely familiar Milky Way and it suddenly struck me that we're all under the same stars. The next time you are feeling a bit lost and lonely, stop. Look up and remember, we're all under the same stars.

---

## Take Action!

1. Know that whatever difficulty you are facing you are NOT alone. Others have faced it and you can, too.

2. Take a moment, take a breath, and ask yourself, "What is the best next step?"

3. Write down a few ways to feel better about the situation and then look up at the sky.

*Remember:* We're all under the same stars. My mother used to say, "The sky is the greatest show on earth." Look up and enjoy the show.

■ ■ ■

## Sometimes the worst place you can be is in your own head."

*Anonymous*

#YouAreNotAlone

**P.S.** Remember: "All is well, all is well. All is perfectly well and unfolding as it will."

29

# Confusion Is the Step Before Clarity

**Q.** How do you make good decisions quickly?

**A.** Try A better? B better?

"Confusion is the step before clarity." Those are the words my eye doctor said when he was playing a game with me that I don't like. Have you ever played this game? I call it the "A better B better game."

I was having my eyes examined, and the eye doctor said, "Which is better? Is A better or B better?"

I said "B"

Then he said, "Which is better? Is A better or B better.

I said, "B"

Then he said, "Which is better? Is B better or A better?"

I said, "A" After a while I started to get confused.

The next time he asked, I said emphatically, "I don't know anymore. I can't tell. I'm so confused!"

He then excitedly said, "Good!"

Surprised, I asked, "Why do you say, "Good" when I am telling you that I'm confused?"

You know what he said? He said, "Because confusion is the step before clarity."

I said, "I didn't come in for this. I came in to get my prescription." Seemed to me that he was being too philosophical.

He went on to explain that making a decision during the eye exam between A and B is very easy in the beginning, because there are obvious choices. But as he narrows in on the right prescription, the choices get closer and closer—to the point at which they are so close that it actually doesn't matter which is better because either will suffice. That made sense.

After this experience it struck me that his words, "Confusion is the step before clarity" are invaluable. That concept is useful in business and in life, because it's so easy to get confused when doing anything new, like starting a new job, learning a new computer program, working with a new client, taking on a new project, or simply coming back from vacation or a few sick days off.

What happens when the confusion sets in? Most people start to feel incompetent, inadequate, stupid, frustrated, upset, angry—rarely anything good. I presented this concept at a leadership summit soon after I heard it, and one of the directors said that quote alone made it worth coming to the meeting because: "What you're saying is that confusion is a step. It is part of the process. When you think of it as a 'step,' as opposed to something that just happens to you that makes you want to stop or quit or get upset over, it gives you the mindset (the peace of mind, the wherewithal) to keep going."

The director said, "I'm definitely planning on sharing this with my leadership team and having them tell their associates. I can see how this can have a positive impact on productivity, revenue growth, and reduction in turnover. It takes the frustration, stress, and discouragement out of the equation when you discover that confusion is a step."

I liked his analysis and immediate implementation. Confusion *is* the step before clarity and it will help you immeasurably if you tell yourself this whenever you encounter anything new or confusing. It will help you press on.

## THE CHANGE SUCCESS FORMULA

Step 1. You try something new.

Step 2. You may get confused.

Step 3. You figure it out.

---

### Take Action!

1. Think of something that has been difficult for you to do that you have been procrastinating about.

2. Set aside some time to take another look at it, knowing "confusion is a step before clarity."

3. Stick with it patiently while trying to figure it out. Once you figure it out, let others know about the value of this concept.

■ ■ ■

## When nothing is sure, anything is possible!

*Dame Margaret Drabble, English novelist, biographer, and critic*

## Never, never, never give up!

*Sir Winston Churchill, former British Prime Minister*

#BeKindToYourself #YouWillFigureItOut

**P.S.** All good things come to those who go after them! Or if at first you don't succeed, then skydiving is definitely not for you! Just kidding. If at first you don't succeed, try, try again!

# 30

# AMERICA'S GOT TALENT AUDITION

**Q.** Do you have what it takes to audition for *America's Got Talent?*

**A.** Yes! (If I can do it, you certainly can do it!)

Part of having more Joy in Business is doing fun and fascinating things with friends and family during your free time to rejuvenate your spirit and then have interesting stories to share from new experiences. Here is one of mine.

Have you ever watched *America's Got Talent*? It's an inspiring and fascinating show where different people with different talents perform in front of the legendary Simon Cowell from *American Idol* fame and a handful of other judges. I was watching back-to-back episodes of the most exciting acts on YouTube one morning, the ones that give you chills or bring tears to your eyes because they are so inspirational. I thought to myself, "I could do that! I would love to audition for *America's Got Talent*, go to Radio City Music Hall, and win the million-dollar prize!"

Then reality set in. I wondered how one goes about doing that. The first place I thought to look was on the website. On it was a list of audition cities, dates, and requirements. The closest city to me was New York City. The venue was the Jacob Javits Center. It was December 17, and I was going to be in town. So far so good!

My daughter Mackenzie was 15 at the time. Do you happen to have teenagers in your world? They don't seem to want to talk to anybody over 16, let alone do anything with them. (That would include moms like me.) I had thought that Mackenzie and I could do fun things together at her age. But it was hard to excite her or convince her to do much of anything with her mom. So I floated the idea. I said I was thinking of auditioning for *America's Got Talent* and asked whether she would be interested in joining me at the Jacob Javits Center on December 17.

This got her attention. She did a double take as if she wasn't sure she had heard me correctly and said, "Wait, what?" (Classic current teen talk.)

I said, "I am thinking of auditioning for *America's Got Talent* and I was wondering if you'd like to come with me on the audition."

She responded, "Mom, I don't mean to be rude in any way, but if you don't mind me asking, what exactly is your talent?"

I said, "On the application they have two sections that I actually could qualify for."

"What are they?"

"One is comedian." I informed her that I have taken many comedy classes in the past and that I am a thought leader and keynote speaker on positive change who happens to be funny. Also, many years ago, I had done open mic in New York City at Standup New York and various other clubs. Honestly though, I don't think of myself as a comedian. I didn't think I would be selected if that was my audition. I told her that I am far more successful with my comedy when people don't expect me to be funny, as in my motivational and inspirational speaking engagements.

But there was another section on the application that I fit into perfectly! It was called "variety." I could be a variety act because that would give me the freedom to do whatever I wanted. I thought that was perfect because in variety I just had to be entertaining, and didn't have to specify the category as clearly. Mackenzie decided she would come with me to the audition.

The guidelines stated that I had to be an American citizen, over the age of 18, who was not running for political office. Check, check, and check! I also had to agree that the producer has final say on who was picked. Check! And sign here. ... Submit and done!

Do you also fit these requirements? Then you too could audition for AGT!

Maybe the thought never crossed your mind. Maybe you have absolutely no interest in doing so. The point is to connect with people, especially precious family members, sometimes an exciting, enticing adventure is a good way to go. It was exciting, fun, and free! (It also turned out unexpectedly to be a great way to strengthen rapport with many of my clients. Texting them "selfies" from the grand ballroom made for enhanced client engagement for sure. Everyone seemed to text back quickly with questions and suggestions.)

"Good news!" I told Mackenzie on our morning drive to school. My online application was accepted. My audition number is 1312631 (see Figure 30.1). So On December 17, Mackenzie and I drove an hour to New York City and, along with 4,000 other hopefuls, we went through the metal detector and registration line. We were directed to a waiting room where we waited for three hours with a colorful assortment of America's best talent!

**Figure 30.1**    Of course BOB, the epitome of flexible and adaptable attended my *America's Got Talent* audition.

There was a cool-looking guy with dreadlocks playing Hendrix in the corner and a cappella singing groups in the hall harmonizing beautifully. We made friends with Torey and her mom Jennifer who had driven all night from their hometown in Ohio to audition (see Figure 30.2).

**Figure 30.2**    Torey, her mom Jennifer, and BOB.

Torey came running over to me and said, "I heard that your audition is like mine, speaking. I'm so glad I found someone who isn't singing or dancing. Let's practice together." And we did. Mackenzie and I met the NuWave gospel singing group. They were really good! We watched a very attractive lady from Ukraine, who played the violin like no other, practicing in the hall. Sweet music and lively dancing permeated from every corner of the room. Exciting and lively conversations among former strangers were everywhere!

There were about 30 different "holding rooms" with approximately 100 people in each, where we were to wait for our auditions. Once we were brought into the actual audition room, a producer and a cameraman sat at a long table in the front. Chairs along the side wall were where we were instructed to sit.

There were about 20 of us, seven acts accompanied by family and friends. The adrenalin was starting to rise. We each had 90 seconds to show our stuff!!

The violinist was slated to go first, but because her violin was electric, she needed a plug and started to get a little upset. As she searched for a power source, a nine-year-old boy got stage fright and kept starting and stopping. His parents encouraged him, and he made it through his routine.

The violinist was still not ready, so I was called next! Mackenzie wished me luck and I launched into my performance. I gave everyone a BOB (my little yellow stress guy. The producer and cameraman loved BOB.) and went into my routine about being flexible and adaptable like BOB. They all laughed and gave BOB a stretch. I mentioned that if I was selected, everyone at Radio City Music Hall would receive a BOB (all 6,015 of them). I showed the funny slides I use in my keynote presentations. Everyone was laughing and learning. Even Mackenzie! The 90 seconds flew by.

When I was finished everyone clapped and cheered. The producer thanked me. The cameraman gave a thumbs up. One of the NuWave singers said, "You were great! You ought to do a TED Talk. (I took her advice and the following March did a TEDx.) It was time for the violinist to perform. She was now worried and started fussing about the cord being in the way and the area being too small.

The producer blurted out, "You need to be more flexible and adaptable like BOB!" Everyone laughed. I nearly died, I was so stunned! The NuWave Gospel singers performed after the electric violinist and then POOF. It was over. We were told that we would be contacted by February with their decisions.

As we were leaving the Javitz Center, we bumped into the dad of a boy in our group who had done a dance routine (he was a professional Broadway type kid). I asked how his son thought he did. He smiled and said, "He thinks he did well. … Because we are flexible and adaptable!" as he dashed up the steps. I said, "Wait!" And threw some extra BOBs to him. He was funny. If nothing else, I was able to spread some joy at the audition.

I knew it was a long shot to be picked, let alone win the milliondollar prize, but I thought there was a chance I could be selected as the funny illogical choice like William Hung on *American Idol*.

You may remember William better as the "She bang" guy. That was the song he sang. She bang, she bang, very off key. He had no professional training but gave his best performance and went viral. Since his audition, Hung, a former civil engineering student at the University of California, Berkeley, has released three albums and appeared on all the major talk shows. He now works as a motivational speaker, telling his audiences that you can't be afraid of people telling you no. You can't be afraid of rejection, of being shamed, or being wrong—because nobody is going to be perfect.

Even though *America's Got Talent* is back on the air for the new season and I didn't receive an email, text, or call, I did have a wonderful time, bond with my daughter, meet incredibly talented, optimistic, and hopeful people, and as an unexpected business benefit, I was able to build deeper relationships with clients by sharing the unique experience of doing something different from the rest. The audition story is definitely a conversation piece that is engaging and fun to share with clients and prospects!

## Take Action!

1. Be bold!
2. Think of something interesting, different, or fun to do.
3. Do it!

■ ■ ■

**It takes courage to grow up and become who you really are.**

*e. e. cummings, American poet, painter, essayist, author, and playwright. (Can you imagine how many picayune grammarians and English teachers tried to make him capitalize his name?)*

#EnjoyTheJourney

**P.S.** Nothing ventured, nothing gained.

# 31

# CRAZY CALLS

## THE WHITE HOUSE STORY (PART 1)

**Q.** Have you ever thought of reaching out to someone but talked yourself out of it because it was crazy?

**A.** Do it anyway!

# THE WHITE HOUSE
# STORY (PART 1)

Can you imagine cold calling the White House and getting the business? If you have ever had a crazy thought to call someone out of the norm, use LinkedIn to connect with someone beyond your realm of possibilities, or seek an outlandish introduction, did you do it? If someone made a crazy suggestion that you contact someone who was in a different stratosphere, would you? That's how I was invited to speak at the White House at the age of 19, by cold calling the president.

For spring break when I was a college freshman, my mother said she wanted me to come home and learn how to sell. I asked, "Why do I need to learn how to sell? I'm a psychology major."

She responded, "Because, without sales you have nothing."

I agreed, came home from the University of Miami, and went to the offices of Baldridge Reading and Study Strategy, Inc., in Greenwich, Connecticut, a speed reading and study skills organization my parents had founded.

When I arrived I asked my mom, "What do you want me to do?"

"I want you to make some cold calls."

"OK, who do you want me to call?"

"Why don't you start with the Catholic schools. Call the nuns and see whether they are interested in a speed reading program."

She gave me a list, a phone, and a short script. My first thought was that this was going to be easy because nuns were religious and would be nice. I was wrong. They may be religious, but they were not very nice. Every one of them abruptly said she was not interested, and a few requested that I not call again. I was crushed. I told my mom that I had failed at sales, that I was not able to get any appointments. They all said no.

She replied, "I'm not interested in the recent past."

"The recent past?" I asked. "This was just a few minutes ago."

She went on: "I'm more interested in the future. I have a more important call for you to make."

"Who do you want me to call now?" I asked.

"The president." She said.

"The president of what?" I asked.

"Our country." She replied.

I exclaimed, "Why? Why are we calling the president?" I will always remember her answer.

"Because he **needs** us!" she said.

I thought she had lost her mind. "How do you know?" I asked.

"Look!" she said. She opened the *New York Times* and pointed to a direct quote. The president said that he wished he could read faster like John F. Kennedy did. My mother wholeheartedly believed that this was a hot lead.

She told me: "Please call him."

"Do you have his number?" I asked.

"Yes, it's public because it's government." She said as she handed me the phone number of the White House.

So I called the president. He wasn't there, but somebody answered and said to "Send information." I did and then went back to college, happy I was not in the working world yet.

Six months later a call came in to the Baldridge Learning Center from the White House. My mother's assistant, who was a little hard of hearing, called my mom on the intercom and said, "Lila, you have a call on Line 2. I think they said it was the Lighthouse. The Lighthouse for the Blind. Don't we support that foundation?"

My mother said, "Yes, we do. Each year we buy light bulbs for their fundraiser. Please let them know that I'm in a meeting and a little too busy to come to the phone right now, but that we wholeheartedly support them, and we will take a case of light bulbs."

So that's what we told the White House when our big moment came. "We wholeheartedly support you and we will take a case of light bulbs."

The White House representative asked, "Are you sure she is too busy to take the call? I am calling from the White House in Washington, D.C., on behalf of the president of the United States." Well, she took the call, and the Baldridges went to Washington!

Please remember this story the next time you make a mistake or feel embarrassed about something. At least you didn't mistake the White House for the Lighthouse.

## Take Action!

1. Look for outrageous opportunities to seize. They are every-where once you look for them.

2. Think even bigger.

3. Go for It! Reach out and see what happens. The White House needed us. Who needs you?

■ ■ ■

**Somewhere someone is looking for exactly what *you* have to offer.**

*Louise Hay, American motivational author of New Thought self-help books*

■ ■ ■

**Life is either a daring adventure or nothing at all.**

*Helen Keller, American author, humanitarian, political activist, and lecturer*

#MakeTheCallAndHaveABall

# 32

# FOLLOW THE HUNCH

**Q.** When is the best time to follow a hunch?

**A.** The critical time is now!

# SEE WHERE IT LEADS

## THE SHIELD STORY

While in London on business I stopped by Westminster Abbey's gift shop and saw family shield magnates. Impulsively, I bought a shield for every name that I personally knew. All were last names of friends, except one was a client. Upon my return I mailed all the shields, along with a "thinking of you" note, except the one for Leslie, my client. It sat on the windowsill of my office for days, weeks, and then months. I would see it and then get busy, feeling a bit strange sending it to her.

Finally, one day I looked at the shield and said to myself, "Either mail it or throw it away." I decided to mail it. Weeks went by afterward and I didn't hear anything, so I gave Leslie a call. She thanked me for the shield, said it was beautiful, and that I was incredibly thoughtful. She went on to say that she was researching her family heritage and didn't know there was a family shield. I asked whether she was still in charge of training. She said no, but she would find out who was.

Three weeks later, on a follow-up call she said, "Don't give up on me. I'm still working on it." Another three weeks passed before an introductory email arrived. It connected me with the new HR director. We met. A few months later, I was brought in. She signed the contract and then was gone. Her replacement initiated an extensive training program in 19 North American markets in six weeks. After the success of this program we did two more tours for reinforcement, retention, and further skill advancement, totaling 57 sessions, grossing a tremendous amount of revenue. All because of a royal family shield that was almost thrown (no pun intended) away.

## Take Action!

1. What action can you take on a gut feeling today?

2. Can you send someone something fun or interesting that will make his or her day?

3. Send it and see what happens.

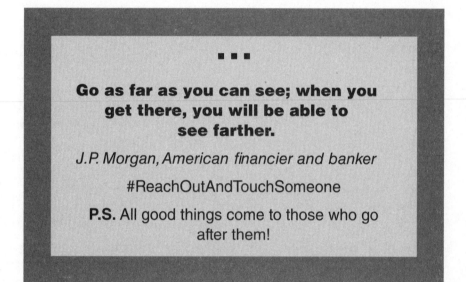

■ ■ ■

**Go as far as you can see; when you get there, you will be able to see farther.**

*J.P. Morgan, American financier and banker*

#ReachOutAndTouchSomeone

**P.S.** All good things come to those who go after them!

## 33

# CARPE DIEM!

**Q.** Do you notice opportunity when it serendipitously appears?

**A.** Start looking for it. It can be in places that will surprise you.

# Seize the Day by Seizing the Opportunity!

There is almost always more to a coincidence than most people think. If you take a deeper look into coincidences that you notice, and act on them, astounding things can result. Being prepared to seize opportunity is a very good business and career model.

## The Island Story

While reading the *New York Times*, one of my clients in private banking noticed that there was a new corporate office opening in New York City for a company whose headquarters was in Vancouver, Canada. As he read, he noticed that the chairman was from the small island off the west coast of Canada that he was from. He decided to seize an opportunity by calling the chairman using that connection.

He called and left a message welcoming the chairman to New York City. He mentioned that he too was raised on Gabriola Island and that they probably knew a lot of the same people. When his call was returned, the conversation started with questions about who knew whom from their mutual island upbringing. Being from such a small place, they knew a lot of the same people.

Eventually, the topic turned to business. My client offered to arrange a meeting to discuss attractive lending opportunities he had to offer. He obtained an appointment and eventually a new client for lending and also investing. It turned out to be a very lucrative and enjoyable relationship.

When you notice and seize the opportunities from coincidences, you have a greater possibility of success.

## The Beverage Story

While on a flight from Milwaukee, Wisconsin, to Nashville, Tennessee, John was excited that he was finally going home from a long business trip. He boarded the plane and settled in. His plan was to relax and enjoy the flight. He wasn't in the mood to speak to anybody.

The pre-flight routine was going smoothly. The pilot came on the PA system with a friendly greeting and optimistic weather report. Seat belts were buckled as safety instructions were given. Once airborne, the fight attendant headed down the aisle with the beverage cart.

The cart stopped next to John and Joe (the person sitting next to him). Suddenly the combustion from one of the carbonated beverages went berserk. Coke started spraying everywhere. Everyone was extremely upset except John and Joe, who both started laughing. It turns out that they were both in the beverage industry. They had an enthusiastic conversation that lasted the rest of the flight. They exchanged business cards—and a new business opportunity was born!

Sometimes the planets align, and surprising things happen if you connect the dots and seize them. Has that ever happened to you?

---

## Take Action!

1. Pay attention.

2. Make connections by asking questions.

3. Make new friends by exchanging contact information and keep in touch. Follow-through is key!

■ ■ ■

**You've got to seize opportunity if it is presented to you.**

*Clive Davis, American record producer and music industry executive*

#GoForIt!

**P.S.** "Even if you're on the right track, you still get run over if you just sit there," Will Rogers, stage and motion picture actor, humorist, columnist, and social commentator.

# 34

# THE BEST SALES INTERVIEW QUESTIONS AND ANSWERS

**Q.** Ever wish you knew the secret to successful interviewing?

**A.** Read on and you will!

The following is a blog post I wrote for Sales Hackers, which is focused on building and shaping the future of sales through educational, actionable, and unbiased content and events. I felt compelled to include it in this book because I truly believe that everyone who is in business is in sales. You are either selling yourself or your organization.

The times you have to sell yourself most are to a future employer for a new career opportunity and to your current employer to keep your career path moving in the right direction. These interview questions are useful to management and corporate leaders as well as human resource and recruiters who want to ask better questions to hire better fits. As you read this chapter, think of how it can help you or someone you know prepare more effectively and successfully for an interview, whether asking or answering the questions.

Even if you are not in sales, you can still gain wisdom from this piece. Watch for way to use portions of it by tweaking the questions and answers to make them your own. They can work for a variety of interviewing scenarios beyond sales (Salt the Hay! Chapter 3).

## SALES HACKER BLOG POST

Have you ever "nailed it!" when interviewing for a sales position? All the stars aligned. Your answers were spot on, and the rapport was effortless. Isn't that the best feeling?! How do you usually feel when interviewing for a sales position?

Excited? Nervous? Confident? Uncertain? Driven? All of the above?

Regardless, there are concrete ways that you can increase your interviewing skills by becoming aware of the questions you will be asked and some effective ways to answer them.

Below are a wide variety of interview questions, ranging from basic to advanced, and high potential answers based on my 15 years of experience as a professional sales recruiter and sales employment agency owner. During that time, I interviewed more than 6,000 sales candidates and placed close to 1,000 in sales positions.

My purpose in sharing this information is for you to make it your own by focusing on the questions and answers that will be of most use to you. Feel free to make changes to suit your interviewing style and scenarios. Remember that there is no one "right" answer to the majority of interview questions you will be asked. Chemistry and gut instinct are beyond our control. So control the controllables to gain insight into the process and increase your chances for success.

## INTERVIEW Q & A

1. **Tell me a little bit about yourself.**

   Danger! Don't go on, and on …. and on about yourself. Stick to the core information, the relevancy of who you are, and the position you are after. For instance, you can say, "I'm from a family of driven entrepreneurs who taught me to go after what I want, and to never give up. In college, I worked to minimize student loans and studied business because I'm fascinated by it (or liberal arts, to get a well-rounded background, or theater because I love acting, or political science, because of the strategy involved in politics)." You can add athletic ability by saying, "I am an avid runner and competitive water skier," or whatever works for you. Mention any sales/sales management success you have had. Again, be brief, genuine, speak your truth, make it interesting, be present, and be passionate.

   Highlight your work experience with specifics. For example: "I am great at new business development. I tripled the client base in my territory in the first year, yielding revenue gains of over $1.2 million" or "I won the top sales incentive trip the last three years" or "As a manager, I am really good at developing people. I doubled the number of sales reps on my team and led them to revenue growth of over 75% last year" or "I'm excellent at relationship building and leveraging sales. One example is when I …" or "I am very good at going after new business" or "I love a challenge, like when. …" Give examples to give substance to who you are and why they should hire you.

2. **Can you tell me more about your sales experience?**

   "Sure." Keep it positive but realistic. Cite what you have specifically done to get sales, such as turn a no into a yes, made the choices you did regarding the companies you worked for.

3. **Why do you want (did you choose) a sales career?**

"I want/chose a sales career because sales is one of the few professions where your hard work, strategic thinking, thorough preparation, and perpetual action literally pay off. It's fun and at times frustrating, challenging, lucrative, and rewarding work."

4. **What is your best memory of a sale you won?**

"The best memory of a sale I won was when I was able to win the sale against all odds." (Hint: Prospective employers want "resilient go-getters.") A brief story is a good way to go. Here is a sample: "Each meeting was getting closer to the commitment and then (mention a few specific obstacles you overcame) the client had to take a medical leave of absence, his replacement was hard to reach, it seemed like priorities were shifting, and the sale was slipping away. I realized I had to get more strategic in my approach so I suggested. ... The hard-won sales are the most rewarding to me." This example shows that you are excited by the challenge of a sale and winning the business. It shows your tenacity, as opposed to highlighting the easy sale that actually isn't considered "real sales" by most. It's considered order-taking.

5. **What was a mistake you made? What did you learn from it?**

"A mistake I made was talking too much. I learned to ask questions to understand more of the thought process of the customer, and learned the importance of when to stop talking." (If you stop talking after this brief answer, it proves you learned how to stop talking!) This answer is also good for the dreaded "What are your weaknesses?" question. You can say that listening is something you feel can always be improved. How about a multiple-choice question like my friend Dustin asks? He is a sales manager in telecommunications. The next question is his.

6. **Put the following three words in order of importance to you. He goes on to say "There is no right answer."**

Money, Recognition, Promotion

Promotion, Recognition, Money

Recognition, Money, Promotion, etc.

What order would you put these three words in to be successful and why? I personally said my answer would be Money, Recognition, Promotion, because if I make the company, my clients, and myself a lot of money, the recognition and promotion will follow in that order. Although Dustin said there is no right answer, his thinking is that if you get recognition, it will motivate you to work hard and earn a promotion, and the money will follow. With a question like this, as long as you have a logical answer, and sincerely mean it, you should be fine.

7. **What do you do to regroup and recover when you have a bad day?**

One sales VP told me that a candidate he hired said that when she had a tough day she would go for a long, fast ride on her horse and leave it all behind. Of course, you could say you go to the gym, since most of us don't have a horse! A trickier question along this line is: "Describe an example of bad day, and how you dealt with it." It's trickier because it is revealing as to what your perception of a bad day is. You can always say you don't dwell on the bad days. You determine what you can learn from them and move on.

8. **How do you motivate yourself?**

Being goal-oriented, money-motivated, self-managed, self-determined, and passionate about sales are all good answers. Many sales leaders have told me they like a person who has a lot of financial responsibility. One answer a sales VP said he liked was when a candidate said, "My mortgage motivates me."

9. **What type of work environment do you like most to do your best work?**

Keep in mind the work environment you are applying for first. Are you OK being in close quarters on the phone tele-selling, or are you best independent and love field sales work? You may want to be proactive and ask the interviewer to describe the type of work environment of the position, as well as the team and his/her management style so you can answer the question more effectively.

10. **Describe your favorite boss and what made him or her your favorite.**

   Caution! Be careful with this one. You can still be honest and careful like this:

   "My favorite boss and I had a great relationship. I didn't like to be micromanaged, so initially I said, 'If you leave me alone, I will make you money.' I had a lot of experience, and a proven track record. He agreed. But I realized that I was being more of a maverick than a team player and, after a while, we adjusted that expectation. He felt the team could learn from me and I agreed. We both thought I could learn from them, even though I was in major accounts. So the work relationship evolved in a different and even better way."

11. **Have you ever had a manager you didn't like? Why was that?**

   This is another tricky and revealing question. If you had a manager from Hell, you can say so, as long as you speak factually, and not negatively, about the person. Separate the person from the behaviors. A disorganized, negative, and indecisive manager makes sense to be awful! Don't mention personal digs, such as he or she was annoying, lazy, impossible, a drunk, or flirtatious, because these words are judgmental, less factual, and more emotional and can sound like you are bashing the manager and thus can backfire. The "why" to that question becomes obvious, but you can say, "The morale of the department started to decline, and inevitable turnover happened, so it was time to go."

12. **When did you first know sales was for you?**

   What they are looking for here is if you have an innate interest in sales. A story (always true) is good here. Whether you had a lemonade stand, worked in your mom's retail store, started a company in your garage, or applied to be on *Shark Tank*, like my daughter's friend, who at the age of 12 got Barbara Corcoran to be his business partner, a short story works well here. Or maybe sales came to you later in life by studying it in college, or selling t-shirts for your fraternity, or when you stumbled upon a blog about sales.

**13. Did you finance any of your college tuition?**

I've heard some sales managers ask this, mostly of fresh grads, to see whether they have had to work for something versus getting a free ride. It's a simple yes or no question. Some say they worked summers or part-time if they didn't have to pay for college. It's not a deal breaker.

**14. What are you most proud of?**

This question lets the interviewer know what you value about your past experiences. It's an opportunity to speak about accomplishments. Practice answering this in a brief and meaningful way before the interview so that you give an answer that is meaningful. Examples: "I most value my five years at XYZ company because it gave me a solid successful sales foundation." Or you can make it more personal like this: "I am most proud of helping my brother get through college because our parents couldn't afford to pay for it, and it completely changed his future for the better" or "I'm most proud of my work on the board of ABC foundation because of the impact we have had on funding life-changing programs."

**15. What is the best advice you have ever received?**

One candidate in an interview for a national advertising sales position said that her father gave her the best advice. He told her "There is always money for a great idea." Keeping that in mind has made her a lot of money selling advertising campaigns and concepts.

**16. What do you do for fun?**

Say what you do for fun. "I scuba dive, compete in Iron Man races, play the drums in a band at local events, do yoga. ..." Again, practice is key. Take a moment right now and answer this question aloud a few times. Collect your thoughts. Say it again and evaluate. Why would you do this on such a simple question? Do it on all the questions listed in this piece. The first answer, even to the simplest question, can come out disjointed and garbled.

**17. How do you balance work and life?**

"I am pretty good at balancing work and life. I am able to leave the day behind me and shift gears to spend time with friends and family" or "I'm terrible at balancing work and life. Work gets the best of me. I am always thinking of the next step in moving the needle in sales" or "I'm great at balancing work and life; funny thing is, when I'm not working, I still find that I meet people who serendipitously lead to sales opportunities."

18. **What have you done that has beat the odds?**

Describe a time in your life when things weren't going well and how you were able to turn it around, for example: "2009 was an awful year. It seemed everyone was in a holding pattern waiting to see what would happen next. The market bottomed out at 6,507.4 in March of that year. Unthinkable!" (You can ask the interviewer: "*How did you do during the recession?*") You can continue by saying: "Some did well. My strategy was to keep making calls and meeting people. I knew at some point the tide would have to turn. "Maintain the Campaign" was one of my senior manager's mottos. It worked! Some panicked. It didn't seem to help them. Eventually, sales opportunities started to come back again. I don't get distracted by the external circumstances that can panic most people. I know activity brings sales."

19. **Describe how/if you are a team player.**

I'm a team player because I think the team can strengthen those on it if they collaborate and commit to helping one another succeed. I also like having the independence to get out of the office and grow my territory.

20. **What are three things you would do to build rapport with people?**

"First, listening is key. Second, asking questions to get to know them better and so I can really pay attention to and care about what they say. Third would be making a connection by talking about what interests them and any insights or experiences I can offer to add value to what they like, need, or want."

21. **What is the first thing you would do when sales are down?**

"When sales are down, I stay highly focused and organized. I create a strategic outreach plan. The plan is focused on consistency and targeted activity numbers. For example: Make 20 phone calls to past and high potential clients. Send 30 emails each day that are directly related to growing new and existing business opportunities, and start going after securing more meetings/appointments."

**22. How do you know you can sell?**

"Because I have done it successfully. I like how the numbers tell the story, so you always know how you are doing" or "Because I love it! It's never boring."

**23. Sell me this pen.**

Has anyone ever asked you to do that? I've had candidates who have been asked this question. You answer it by doing a needs analysis. *Don't* answer by going on and on about the features and benefits of the pen and why the person should buy it! *Do* ask, "What kind of pen do you like to write with?" *Do* ask, "Describe your favorite pen. What does it look like? How does it write? Thick, thin, smoothly? What color ink do you prefer? Do you care about the way it looks, or just the way it writes? Where are you going to use it? Out with a client or in the office? What price range/ballpark are you looking to spend? What else do you like about your favorite pen?" Then provide the reasons the person will like the pen you are selling/or not like it, depending on the answers to your probing questions. Check in with a question like: "What do you think about this pen? Would you like to purchase it today? Cash or charge? If no, why not? What would be better suited for you? Is that what you would like to buy instead? OK. I'll order you one now." (Remember to close at the end!)

**24. How do you handle disappointment?**

"Learn what I can from it, and move on." Short and sweet! If he or she asks, "That's it?" say "Yes!" I have seen far too many team members waste valuable selling time venting about the "what if's" of a sale that didn't happen, when instead it would have been a better use of their time to get back out there.

## Strange Questions

Every once in a while, during my experience as a professional recruiter, a candidate would tell me that a sales manager, or a top executive, asked a strange or blunt question. If you can prepare to expect the outrageously unexpected question, you will have more success. When asked a strange question, take a moment to think, and then answer. Here are a few:

**What color best describes you and why?** One sales manager said he asked this question because it can't be rehearsed. For an answer, he liked to hear things like this: "Red because I am bold" or "Green because it's the color of money and I am money-motivated" or "Yellow, because I am very optimistic." There is no "right" answer to this question. He said he liked to see how candidates think on their feet and justify their answers.

**What animal would you say you are most like and why?** The answer the candidate gave to this strange question was a cheetah because they are one of the smartest and indisputably the fastest animal in the jungle. He went on to say he likes to do a quick analysis of a situation and get things done! (Like a cheetah would.) The key here is to play along and not get tense, flustered, or feel any pressure to give the perfect answer, because there is none. Just smile and do your best.

Are you prepared for the last interview question? Here it is.

**25. Do you have any questions?**

Yes! You'd BETTER have a few questions because questioning shows interest. But don't ask questions for the sake of asking questions. Ask questions on things you are curious about. Below are a few questions that the candidates who were most successful in getting sales career offers asked. Of course, you don't have to ask all of them. Ask the ones you want to know the answers to. FYI: Questions 1, 5, and 6 are very impressive to prospective employers. The candidates I prepped to answer these questions almost always received the offer.

1. Describe your best SDR/AE/Sales Manager/Director/Executive. What characteristics did he/she possess that made him or her so good?

2. What kind of leader are you?

3. How would someone who works for you describe you?

4. What do you expect/value most in the people you manage/lead?

5. What would be a few things that someone you work with, or who works for you, has done or could do that would exceed your expectations?

6. What could a person who worked for you do that would "wow" you?

7. Do you like working here? How successful have you been here, and what do you attribute that success to?

8. What do you/others like most about working here? What could be improved?

9. Can you recall a sale you or someone on your team made that was most memorable? What was it and why?

10. Can you please describe the interview process. How many applicants are you considering and how do I compare? What will be the determining factor in making an offer?

11. [When] Can we set up the next interview?

12. What timing works best for you to meet again?

---

## Take Action!

1. Review the questions in this chapter before any interview.

2. Write additional questions you anticipate being asked.

3. Write out a variety of different responses to the questions you anticipate and then read them aloud. Preparation is key!

■ ■ ■

**Find out what you like doing best and get someone to pay you for it.**

*Katherine Whitehorn, British journalist, writer, and columnist known for her wit and humor*

#Interviews = Showtime!

**P.S.** My mother used to say, "Without sales you have nothing!" To test that theory, I recently asked my friend Ann, who has a very impressive financial background and is a very successful comptroller for one of the big broadcast networks in New York City, what career advice she would give a recent graduate or someone transitioning in a career.

Her answer: "Go into sales!"

"Why?"

"Because sales is where all the money is."

But if you do what you love, the money will follow, too.

# 35

# INTERVIEWING ESSENTIALS

**Q.** What's the key to successful interviewing?

**A.** Become an MPA. Always go for the offer. Practice the three interviewing essentials.

# 1. Become an MPA

Being a sales recruiter for 15 years, I learned early on that my goal was to find or create MPAs (most placeable applicants) if I wanted to be successful at my straight commission recruiting career. (Net-net I broke all prior sales records and ranked number 1 every year out of 98 recruiters.)

To be or become an MPA you must: Be your best, look your best, and prepare your best. Then relax, have fun, and enjoy the process.

You must arrive to interviews early. Practice answering interview questions ahead of time, and follow up afterward. Treat every interview like a sales call and the interviewer like a client.

For more information on becoming an MPA and nailing your next interview, view my Facebook Live recording on this subject: https://www.youtube.com/watch?v=hERSSAvC4yI

# 2. Always Go for the Offer!

Make them want you! You can always say no.

The most heartbreaking part of recruiting was when candidates would go into interviews half-heartedly. Some would go just to check out the company to see whether they liked it, realizing afterward that they really wanted the job, and didn't get it because they didn't sell themselves. I would try to get them back in for a second interview, and the managers would say, "This is a sales position. He/she didn't sell me." "Shopping" is NOT a good way to go. A better way is to always go for the offer—yes, every time, by being your best, giving it your all, having enthusiasm, expressing interest, keeping your answers concise and to the point. Make them want you! Until you have an offer, you have nothing. Often you will not receive an offer on the first interview, but you can close on the next interview. If you decide the next day that it's not for you, you can cancel the next interview, but at least you have given yourself a fair shot.

## 3. Practice, Practice, Practice!

It feels foolish at times practicing with a friend or in front of a mirror answering interview questions. But the payoff is huge. You will interview better. Some worry that if they practice writing down interview answers or saying them prior to the interview that they may sound canned. I call it being "planned, not canned." Once you are prepared, you earn the right to be spontaneous. Winging it is for the birds!

**Three Rules for Interviewing Success**

1. Those who prepare most win, so prepare and practice interview questions before the interview.

2. Those who ask the questions have the power, so prepare and practice asking questions during the interview process

3. People are persuaded by their own words, so practice and prepare to listen to the words that the interviewer uses in order to align with them during the conversation.

## 4. Interviewing for a Sales Position

Interviewing for a sales position is ever-changing. One sales professional recently asked me for tips on doing a Skype interview successfully. My suggestion was to look at the camera instead of the screen. One sales manager advised to do it in a quiet, private place with no distractions in the background. He said he had a Skype interview with one candidate during which he could see and hear cars moving. Using common sense is a good thing! Of course, researching the company and person you are interviewing with is essential. But don't assume anything from what you read. Ask questions to clarify instead of spewing facts to build rapport. Always know why you are interviewing for the job. They will probably ask Why us? and Why you?

## Take Action!

1. Do what it takes to become an MPA—most placeable applicant.

2. Be present by deep breathing.

3. Practice, practice, practice.

■ ■ ■

**Believe in yourself! Have faith in your abilities! Without a humble but reasonable confidence in your own powers you cannot be successful or happy.**

*Norman Vincent Peale, American minister and author best known for his work in popularizing the concept of positive thinking*

■ ■ ■

**The future belongs to those who believe in the beauty of their dreams.**

*Eleanor Roosevelt, former First Lady and American political figure, diplomat, and activist*

#DoYourBestBeYourBest

**P.S.** Successful interviewing is a win/win! You get an awesome job and they get a great talent!

## 36

# THE CRITICAL
# TIME IS NOW!

**Q.** Have you ever looked at your to-do list at the end of the day and noticed that nothing is crossed off?

**A.** To feel a sense of accomplishment, think of something you did that day, write it on the list, and cross it off!

# BUT FIRST, COFFEE

Do you ever wonder where your time goes? How to successfully balance your work and life? Maybe the solution is on a t-shirt I recently read that said: "But first, coffee." Or maybe it's in the time and priority management tips below.

How do you find the time for your daily work commitments, internal and external networking, and still spend enough time with friends and family? You can accomplish all these things and more by discovering how to reclaim your day. The Critical Time is NOW is about creating zones of time to acquire new ways to make the most out of each day.

There is an expression: "Lose an hour in the morning and you'll spend the rest of the day looking for it."

So here is a seven-step strategy designed for you to get more done in less time, with more success and less stress.

## 1. DECIDE WHAT IS MOST IMPORTANT TO ACCOMPLISH

Once you are clear on what you want to do, self-questioning is key. Here are a few examples of self-questioning: "What is the one thing I can do to further my success toward this goal?" Then do it and repeat.

When you ask yourself a question, you get the real answer. It keeps you focused, organized, and building momentum. It also helps you to leave your day feeling more satisfied, because you are taking action toward accomplishing something you want. For example, if you want to live a more balanced life because you are starting to feel like all you do is work, work, work (Have you ever felt this way?), ask yourself: "What's the one thing that I can do to further my success in balancing work and life?" It may be to treat yourself to a walk in the woods after work or take your children on a surprise adventure.

If you want to network more, you can ask yourself: "Who would I like to get to know better in my company or industry? Write down one to three names of people you would like to network with and why. Then email, call, or message each or use LinkedIn to set up a brief coffee meeting, Skype call, or phone chat. Making minor changes leads to major impact when setting and achieving your goals, and it feels terrific.

## 2. Do More Self-Questioning

The following questions provide clarity of thought and focus you toward accomplishing more in your day.

"What's the best use of my time right now?" is a good question to ask yourself at the start of each day. It helps you prioritize your obligations.

Another question as the day goes on is: "Is this the best use of my time right now?" This question keeps you on track, because what you started working on may no longer be the priority, so it is a great way to self-assess how you are spending your time in order to do more of what you really want and need to do.

If you ask yourself the question above and your answer is "No," you can still change course. Because we have a compulsion for completion, we think it will only take a few minutes to complete a task that is not our priority. Unfortunately, it actually takes two to three times longer to do something than you think it will. So if you discover that what you are doing is NOT the best use of your time, it is essential to use a self-command. Say to yourself: "Stop, get to the priority!" or "Stop, shift," write what you are doing on your to-do list so you can do it at another time, and then shift your time and attention to the actual priority.

## 3. Use the Red Ruler

One time-saving tool that can save you three to five hours each week is called the Red Ruler, a technique for recovering from interruptions faster. Did you know that lack of a recovery system for interruptions is the number one time robber? Every time you are interrupted it takes anywhere from 2 to 15 minutes to recover—if you ever recover at all.

Let's do the math. If you are interrupted 60 times in your day with things like email, meetings, calls, or people who stop by, and it takes about 5 minutes to recover from each interruption, 5 minutes times 60 interruptions equals 300 minutes or 5 hours of lost time. Have you ever wondered where the time goes in your day? Ever said to yourself at the end of the day: "I feel like I accomplished nothing"? One guy told me the only thing he crossed off on his to-do list was Monday and he put Tuesday.

But if you have an interruption recovery technique, the recovery time is 2 to 15 *seconds* versus minutes per interruption. Five seconds times 60 interruptions is 300 seconds or only 5 minutes of lost time. Somewhere between 5 minutes and 5 hours is time you can reclaim by using interruption recovery techniques like the Plus, Plus, Dash explained in Chapter 18, and the Red Ruler.

I discovered the Red Ruler while facilitating a time management training session several years ago. A woman in the class said she never has had any problems with interruptions. When I asked why, she said she had a red ruler. I asked, "What do you do, hit people with it?"

She explained, "When an interruption comes while I'm working on something, I take out my red ruler, put it on what I am doing, deal with the interruption and, when I'm finished, I look for the red ruler and get back to the task at hand. The red ruler marks my place like a bookmark, so I can instantly recover." Applying the Red Ruler concept allows you to instantly recover from interruptions. It is a huge time-saving tool!

If you do most of your work on a computer you can flag or highlight where you are so you can go back faster. Give it a try and see how it can work for you.

You truly can have a more balanced existence and reclaim your day, career, and life if you practice any of the ideas above. One of my favorite quotes is *"Those who say it cannot be done should stop interrupting the person who's doing it!"* You can do it! The Critical Time is NOW!

## 4. ZONE YOUR TIME

Zoning involves creating a specific amount of time to do like tasks. A phone zone is making back-to-back calls, an email zone is devoting a specific amount of time to solely attend to emails. The rationale is that *like tasks done together builds momentum.* You can zone any activity. Pick a slot of time in your day. Make an appointment with yourself as if it were an important meeting not to be missed. See how much more productive you will become.

## 5. Request a Response

A client mentioned that she was getting tired of constantly following up with people to finish projects, finding answers to questions, and moving the needle on business opportunities without getting many replies. So she started to experiment with the subject line of the emails she was sending to see which received the best response. It seemed the standard words she put on the subject line, such as "following up" or "checking in" weren't working. When she put "Response Requested" or "Reply Requested" and tested this for a few weeks, she found that she received 60% more replies to her emails.

I mentioned her findings in my time management, sales, and communication skills seminars; several months later those who attended the sessions emailed me to report similar success. Give it a try and see whether it helps you to be more productive and efficient.

## 6. Stop Procrastinating

Do you procrastinate? Honestly, do you ever put things off? Things you should be doing but you didn't do because you just didn't feel like doing, or didn't want to do, or it was too hard to do, so you told yourself that you were going to do it later when you had lots of time. But when do you actually have lots of time? Usually never. Here is a four-step process for anti-procrastination. It's just four words: Look, Divide, Begin, Reward.

1. Look at the scope of what needs to be done.
2. Divide it into doable chunks (something you can do within 2 to 15 minutes).
3. Begin with the first chunk: *"A job begun is half done."* Notice that "begin" is Step 3. Because you can't begin until you look and divide. That's why most procrastinate. They look and panic at the magnitude of the task and then put it aside. That's why *divide* is such a critical part of the anti-procrastination formula.
4. Reward yourself for finishing. Say positive things like "Yes!" or "Done!" or "Damn, I'm Good!" or take a break. Do what works best for you. Self-praise fuels momentum. See Step 7 below:

## 7. Indulge in Self-Praise

Behavior rewarded gets repeated. If you feel you have done a great job and no one is around to give you your well-deserved recognition, give it to yourself. Self-praise, when done sincerely, is very motivational and energizing. Give it a try. (See Chapter 10 or Chapter 17 for more praise words and phrases.)

---

### Take Action!

1. Self-question to stay on track with your time.

2. Zone your time. Like tasks done together builds momentum.

3. Divide tasks into doable chunks and begin with the first chunk.

---

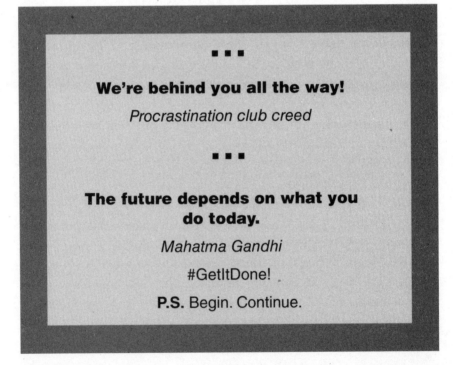

■ ■ ■

**We're behind you all the way!**
*Procrastination club creed*

■ ■ ■

**The future depends on what you do today.**
*Mahatma Gandhi*
#GetItDone!
**P.S.** Begin. Continue.

# 37

# CLUTTER-FREE!

**Q.** Do you ever feel overwhelmed by clutter?

**A.** Join the club. Here's how to conquer it.

Do you have clutter in your life? I have been struggling with what to do with things and "stuff" for decades. I even had mottos such as:

Clutter-free in '93!

It's time in '99!

It's done in 2001!

But you're never really done with clutter it seems, unless you stay on top of it. My friend Simone says clutter blocks the blessings. I agree!

I have been battling clutter most of my life. (Not the hording type of clutter battles, just the paper piles that tend to multiply when I'm busy.) It was so difficult at one point that I actually went to a clutter support group called Messies Anonymous founded by Sandra Felton. She has dedicated her life to helping people win the clutter war. Messies Anonymous has a 12-step program similar to Alcoholics Anonymous. People who are disorganized are called messies. Those who are neat are called cleanies. I was a messie. Each meeting would start with each person introducing him- or herself by saying, "Hi, I'm John B., and I am a messie" (for real).

When I told my friend Jenny about going to my first Messies Anonymous meeting, it was a strange and foreign concept to her. To clarify she asked, "Let me get this straight, in Messies Anonymous, unlike AA, you can drink, but not spill? Is that right?"

She's so funny. "Yes, that's right!" I said.

To help me declutter, I bought many books over the years such as *Clutter Control* by Jeff Campbell, *Clutter Feng Shui* by Karen Kingston, *Clutter's Last Stand: It's Time to De-junk Your Life* by Don Aslett, and the Bible of all decluttering books: *The Life-Changing Magic of Tidying Up: The Japanese Art of Decluttering and Organizing* by Marie Kondo.

Buying all these books, of course, created even more clutter! After all, they have to go somewhere. That's key in decluttering: having "homes" for things. My favorite book title was *Lose 200 Pounds This Weekend* (of clutter, that is) by Don Aslett.

A few days ago, I lost 100 pounds by emptying huge bins of office papers into two black Hefty trash bags. My new best friend is my big box of black Hefty trash bags. I was so determined to get more clutter out of my life that I awoke at 3:00 a.m. and ran straight to the battle-ground, my office. I plowed through the multitude of boxes packed with papers and finished by 7:00 a.m. It happened to be trash pickup day, so I eagerly ran down the driveway with two 50-pound bags of discarded papers. (How did I know they were 50-pound bags? I started my career in the mailroom, which gave me a good feel for weight.)

I ran to the trash bins out by the street and, to my dismay, they had already been emptied. "Oh no!" I thought. "I want these bags out of my life right now!" Just then the City of Stamford recycling truck was coming down the one-way street perpendicular to my home. I flagged it down. The driver said, "Throw them in the back." But I couldn't because it was full. Just then a guy came out of the truck and yelled to the driver to have the trash compactor activated. Cars were starting to pile up behind us—but I was on a mission. A mission to lose 100 pounds this morning no matter what! (Did I mention that I was dressed in my PJs, slippers, and robe while standing in the middle of the street?)

It took a bit of awkward waiting, but the bags made it into the back and were gone. When I started my paper purging project there were 21 boxes to go through. Then 15, then 10, it was torture, but I knew if I kept going they would eventually be gone. Seven more, then five left. I knew there was an end to it if I stuck with it. The hardest part is how dense each pile of papers is and the decisions you must make to keep or toss, shred, burn, or file. Endless questions came up like: "Why do I need it? Where will I put it? How will I find it? Do I really need it? Will I ever use it again? Who else could use it?" I was determined to live a clutter-free life. This was 2017. What rhymes with 2017? Could it be clean in '17? Yes, that works!

Here are the rules to declutter efficiently and effectively:

**Rule 1.** Be flexible and adaptable. AFA All the Way! Always Flexible and Adaptable (Chapter 2).

**Rule 2.** Stop bringing stuff into your home, work, car. Buy less, enjoy what you have more.

**Rule 3.** Devote 30 to 60 minutes minimum each day to sorting, tossing, and donating your stuff.

**Rule 4.** Celebrate small successes.

**Rule 5.** Keep going! No matter how you feel, don't let up. That little voice in your mind needs to say, "You can do this! You got this! instead of Why do I have to do this? Why am I decluttering rather than being outside in the beautiful weather? No one else has this burden. It's so unfair. Oh please! Keep going!

**Rule 6.** Take time to go through every piece of the clutter and decide whether you love it. Do you need it? Do you want to rid your life of it? What would your life be like without it?

**Rule 7.** Make decluttering a daily habit. "Every day throw something away!" There is always a drawer, closet, filing cabinet, computer file, that can use a little time and attention. By making purging a habit, you only need to go through your accumulated stuff once.

**Rule 8.** Put it back! Most clutter comes from taking things out and not putting things back.

**Rule 9.** Appreciate the new space you create. Admire your work.

**Rule .10.** Do it again! Repeat as needed.

**Bonus Golden Nugget:** The Sun Dial. Pick a room or area to organize. Put your arms out elbows touching hands apart forming a V. Only look at what you can see in that V area. Make that area perfect. Pivot to the right and only improve that area. Keep pivoting and improving as you rotate like a sundial to focus your time and attention on what you see in the V. Once you have made a complete 360-degree rotation you are finished. Then go to the next room and repeat.

The messies call this the Mount Vernon method of declutterization, because this is how Mt. Vernon is cleaned and kept so pristine as a national treasure. It works! Give it a try.

---

## Take Action!

1. Pick one of the rules above that you feel will help you tackle your clutter.

2. Try the Sundial/Mt. Vernon method of declutterization.

3. Make a habit of bringing less stuff into your world and tossing regularly.

■ ■ ■

## "Later" is the best friend of clutter...

*Peter Walsh, Australian-American professional organizer, writer, and media personality*

■ ■ ■

## Clutter is nothing more than postponed decisions.

*Barbara Hemphill, expert, author, and authority in removing clutter*

■ ■ ■

## Get rid of clutter and you may just find that it was blocking the door you were looking for.

*Katrina Meyer, bestselling author on lifestyle tips*

#KeepTossing

**P.S.** Control your clutter; renew your life!

# 38

# WHAT'S YOUR
# "ONE THING"?

**Q.** Too much to do? Too little time?

**A.** Focus on the "one thing."

Now that Part 3 of this book is ending, it would be a good idea to reflect on what you have read. Take a moment and flip back through the pages and note below the Golden Nuggets you would like to use before moving on to Part 4.

Is it to know that you are not alone, confusion is the step before clarity, to do something fun and fascinating, make crazy calls, follow hunches to see where they lead, or to practice asking and answering interview questions. Perhaps it's remembering that those who prepare most win, those who ask the questions have the power, and people are persuaded most by their own words. Or could it be using the time tools like the Red Ruler, zoning your time and clutter control. Once your list is complete, rank the top three things you will do differently, and commit to doing your "one thing" today.

**Favorite Golden Nuggets**

_____

_____

_____

My top three Golden Nuggets in order of importance:

1. _____

2. _____

3. _____

The "One Thing" I will commit to do first is:

_____

_____

## Take Action!

1. Ask yourself each business day, "What's the one thing I can do to further my success for tomorrow?"

2. Do it!

3. Leave your day feeling satisfied!

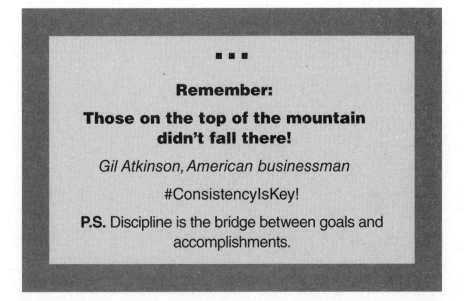

**...**

**Remember:**

**Those on the top of the mountain didn't fall there!**

*Gil Atkinson, American businessman*

#ConsistencyIsKey!

**P.S.** Discipline is the bridge between goals and accomplishments.

# PART 4

# 39

# TAKE ACTION!

**Q.** How can you execute the ideas in this book?

**A.** Select the most useful concepts and formulate and adhere to new expectations.

# Embody the Corporate Culture Code (CCC)

All the Golden Nuggets within these pages are purposefully designed to *make the best even better at increasing revenue and productivity while decreasing frustration and stress.* The key is to use the concepts by creating new expectations with them. This will lead to an evolution of positive culture change.

Expectation setting and monitoring are essential for personal and organizational growth. The formula for success is as follows:

1. Write a list of expectations you want to be part of your team and corporate culture. A good way to determine new expectations is to ask yourself what should be done differently. *Should* is a key word here.

2. Catch yourself when you think or say, they *should* know better or we *shouldn't* be doing this anymore. I call this the "should factor." Notice it and add anything you say "should" about to your expectation list.

3. Once a master expectation list has been developed for everyone to strive for, add a specific expectation section listing additional expectations for each individual based on his or her skill level and background.

   **General Expectations:** A general expectation list is best when created in a brainstorming session with your team. Have the team contribute most of the items. Write the expectations on a white board. Once the team has exhausted their own list, add anything you feel they may have missed. Having the team contribute the items for the list creates buy-in. Most of what they put on the list will be things you probably would put on it, too.

   **Specific Expectations:** The specific expectation list is best when created in a one-on-one meeting with individual team members to help them reach higher goals and aspirations.

An example of an expectation list that uses the Golden Nuggets in this book follows:

1. AFA All the Way: Always Flexible and Adaptable.

2. Breathe! Do the 4–4–6. Inhale, hold, exhale.

3. Salt the Hay and find a way, because behind every two can'ts there is a can.

4. Watch your Ogive.

5. Strive to live in the House of Glad and create House of Glad experiences for your team and customers.

6. Pay your R.E.N.T. every day. Monitor your Rest, Exercise, Nutrition, and Thoughts.

7. Embrace and encourage Purple Breaks. Designate a Purple Break room. Make Purple Breaks part of your culture code.

8. Use the Velvet Hammer words, questions, and phrases.

9. Speak the Language of the Lands. Treat people the way they want to be treated.

10. Introduce and start a Because of You award program.

11. Encourage meditation or quiet time to reflect and recharge.

12. Take the bee stinger out sooner than later. Help each other to take the bee stinger out, too.

13. Remember that confusion is the step before clarity.

14. Make crazy calls.

15. Follow hunches.

16. Seize opportunity.

17. Hire the best.

18. Control clutter.

19. Value time—yours and others—by using the Plus, Plus, Dash and self-questioning.

20. Determine your "one thing."

21. Take action! Agree to and use a culture code by applying and reinforcing these ideas.

## Expectations Must Be

1. In writing.
2. Clear, that is, easy to understand the meaning of each expectation.
3. Mutually agreed upon; a signature of commitment works well here.
4. Visible, posted on a bulletin board, desk, or card.
5. Evolutionary. Review and update as needed.

Once expectations become habits they can be taken off the list and new expectations can be added. Expectations should be reviewed monthly to notice the positive evolution that occurs.

## THE CCC

You can use any of the expectations listed above as a code or new language at work. Below are a few examples of the Joy in Business vernacular you can incorporate into your business world:

- **AFA** is very useful in emails or conversation when someone needs to reschedule or make a change. It is a relief to be on the receiving end of the AFA code. It takes far less time.
- **4–4–6.** Instead of telling someone to take it easy or chill, you can say, "I think we need a 4–4–6." It's code for deep breathing, taking a moment to regroup.
- **Ogive.** If things aren't going as planned, it's easy to get frustrated, but better to tell yourself or others, "I think we are experiencing a bit of Negative Ogive. Let's work toward getting out of it." One manager I Worked with had a sign on his door, "No Negative Ogive Allowed."
- **"Time for a Purple Break,"** is a good way to go after an intense meeting.
- "Let's **Salt the Hay** on that … what can we do now that we have explored a few can't s?"
- How's your **R.E.N.T** coming along?
- "What house are you in? Time to get back to the **House of Glad**."
- "Take the **Bee Stinger** out."

## Take Action!

1. Create a new general expectation master list with your team.

2. Make an individual expectation list, too.

3. Monitor and adjust expectations as needed. Create your Corporate Culture Code.

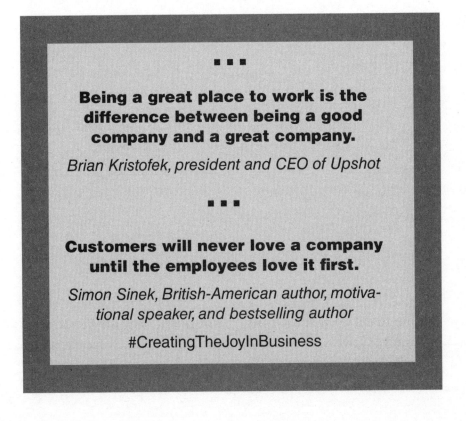

■ ■ ■

**Being a great place to work is the difference between being a good company and a great company.**

*Brian Kristofek, president and CEO of Upshot*

■ ■ ■

**Customers will never love a company until the employees love it first.**

*Simon Sinek, British-American author, motivational speaker, and bestselling author*

#CreatingTheJoyInBusiness

# 40

# THE WHITE HOUSE STORY (PART 2)

**Q.** Have things ever not worked out as planned?

**A.** Adjust your expectations and persevere, or take on the challenge.

When I cold called the White House (see Chapter 31) at the age of 19, I never in my wildest dreams expected to speak there. So the surprise of getting a call back from the White House and going to Washington, D.C. was quite a thrill. But things don't always work out as we think. I never met the president. He wasn't there that day. (Has that ever happened to you? You were excited in anticipation of something about to happen only to find that fate had other plans?)

The assignment I was given was to teach the president's staff how to read his mail faster. Any idea how many letters the president of the United States received each week in 1978, before email? A lot! Up to 40,000. The goal was to respond back within nine days with a staff of 25 people. They exceeded the goal with the speed reading techniques and strategies that we shared. The program was conducted in the Indian Treaty room.

Fast forward to 2015. I'm at a keynote speaker boot camp in Dallas, Texas. I told the White House story on stage in front of 50 other professional speakers and authors to get feedback and perfect it. One of them took me aside at the break and said, "Your White House story is great, but you never met the president."

"I know," I agreed.

She said, "It would be so much better if you did."

I answered, "Yes, but I don't like to think like that, of the what could have or should of happened."

She said, "Well, he's still alive. He's 91 and has brain cancer, but you can still meet him. It would be an even better story if you actually met him." Then she said three words that started the journey, "I challenge you!" She challenged me to meet President Jimmy Carter!

Accepting her challenge, I didn't really know where to start. But I called the Carter Center in Atlanta, Georgia. They said that the best way to meet the president was to attend his church in Plains, Georgia. There was no guarantee he would be there, but that was my best bet. So now all I had to do was drive an hour to JFK airport, fly 2 hours and 32 minutes to Atlanta, rent a car, drive 154 miles from Hartsfield Jackson Atlanta International Airport to Plains (approximately 3 hours), stay overnight, get up at 4:00 a.m. to arrive at the Maranatha Baptist

Church on Georgia Highway 45 North in time to get in line with the 400 plus other people from all over the world who wanted to meet the president.

Since there was no guarantee he would be speaking at church on any given Sunday, I decided to go the Sunday right before Christmas. I had heard that he usually spends Christmas with his family in Plains, so the odds were good that he would be there. Sadly, on that day, December 20, 2015, his grandson had unexpectedly passed away. I wasn't sure whether he would make it, but he did. He was shaken and obviously sad, although he was still able to present the lesson well. I was so sorry for his loss.

After his Sunday school lesson, there were very specific instructions on how to approach the president for a photo opportunity. No talking, no interaction. Be quick and move on.

I said to the organizer, "But I have a very special bond with President Carter. He invited me to speak at the White House during his administration."

She said, "Honey, you see that line over there? *Everyone* in it has a special bond they feel they need to speak to President Jimmy Carter about. *We don't have all day!*" I was determined to speak with him regardless. I waited my turn, took my place beside him, and while smiling through clenched teeth did my best attempt at ventriloquism.

Without moving my lips, I said, "President Carter, I taught speed reading to your staff per your invitation to your White House.

He turned to me with his eyes widened and with a look of awe said, "That was you? I remember bringing in a speed reading company." (He brought in both Baldridge Reading to teach his staff and Evelyn Wood Reading Dynamics to teach his family.) He went on to say, "*You have done a great service to your country by assisting my staff with the efficiency and effectiveness in handling the White House correspondence. Thank you!*"

And poof, the moment was gone. I brought BOB—my flexible and adaptable friend—along to be in the photo. President Carter didn't seem to mind. I also presented him and Rosalynn with the Because of You award (see Chapter 22) for their humanitarian work (see Figure 40.1).

The lesson here is that some goals can happen quickly from out of nowhere, while others can take a lifetime. You can expect something to happen that doesn't, and yet be pleasantly surprised by things you never would have imagined. That's the beauty of life. Enjoy the journey!

**Figure 40.1    BOB and I presenting the Because of You award to Jimmy Carter.**

## Take Action!

1. Challenge yourself to do something daring or different.

2. When things happen differently than you expected or hoped for, curb any disappointment and look for the magic that may follow.

3. Always be on the lookout for new experiences to venture into.

■ ■ ■

**All our dreams can come true if we have the courage to pursue them.**

*Walt Disney, American entrepreneur, animator, voice actor, and film producer*

#BeyondTheNorm

**P.S.** Go for it!

# 41

# IT WILL NEVER
# BE YESTERDAY

**Q.** Do you ever dwell on the past, wishing some things had gone differently?

**A.** Live in the now and make the most of it!

When my son Wilson (see Figure 41.1) was five, he said something quite profound. He was acting restless at bedtime and I told him to calm down or he would be grounded. He wouldn't listen to me. (Do you know any five-year-olds who don't listen?) So I told him he was grounded. His punishment was that he couldn't bring his Scooby-Doo stuffed animal to show-and-tell the next day. He had to take a little rubber frog instead. Well, he was not happy.

The next day when I picked him up from school, I asked how show-and-tell went. He was still upset and said, "It was fine, and I don't want to talk about it!"

I said, "Wilson, if you had just listened to me yesterday...."

He clinched his fists with rage and screamed, "Mom, it will never be yesterday, so why do you keep talking about it?"

I thought that was genius and I wrote it down. I called a client later that day and happened to mention that my son said something I thought was pretty insightful. He said, "It will never be yesterday, so why do you keep talking about it?"

She said, "That's good! You should say that every time you speak. That quote would have saved me 10 years of therapy!"

It's true! It will never be yesterday, so why keep talking about it? It's time to move on.

**Figure 41.1    Wilson Kent McAlarney, age five.**

---

## Take Action!

1. Leave the past behind.

2. Determine what needs to be done.

3. Do it now.

---

■ ■ ■

**You can't start the next chapter of your life if you keep re-reading the last one.**

*Tiny Buddha, a website that provides "simple wisdom for complex lives"*

#BuildABrightFutureNow

**P.S.** Your future is waiting.

# 42

# PERSISTENCE OF PERCEPTION

**Q.** Do you at times look for new landscapes?

**A.** Perhaps it's best to see with new eyes.

Persistence of Perception is when the way you perceive your world stays the same unless you do something to change your perspective. I learned about Persistence of Perception in the laundry room. One day while I was doing laundry, the handle to the dryer fell off in my hand. I asked my husband to help fix it. He had a quick solution. If you turn the handle upside down, slide it back into the slot, pull up and pull back, you can open the dryer door.

It worked! Until the handle completely wore out. I called to him again and said his trick wasn't working anymore. He brought over a screwdriver. He put the screwdriver in the slot, turned it to the right, pulled back, and it created just enough leverage to open the dryer door.

It was an awkward yet doable solution until the screwdriver got lost. I think it may have fallen behind the dryer. Regardless, I called to my husband again and said, "Can't we fix this in a more permanent way?" It was a temporary solution to a permanent problem. (Have you ever used a temporary solution for a permanent problem?)

He had an idea. He came back with a huge magnet and some pliers. He put the magnet on the dryer, straddled the magnet with the pliers, squeezed really hard, pulled back, and the dryer door opened. It worked!

So I used this new system of opening the dryer door to some success for quite a while until a neighbor asked if she could use my dryer because hers was broken. I said, "Sure! Here's how it works. You turn this knob to the temperature that you want, this knob to the time you want, then you take these pliers and straddle this magnet, squeeze hard, and pull back."

She said, "What are you doing?!"

I said, "I'm showing you how to dry your clothes."

She asked, *"Don't you think there's a better way?"*

"YES! But I either need a new dryer or a new husband." We did end up buying a new dryer, and I did keep my husband, but that is a classic case of persistence of perception.

The way you get used to doing things persists unless you stop for a moment and take a step back. Become more aware of the way you work by taking a step outside yourself and observing. That way you can assess how you are doing things and make any necessary changes.

What is the persistence of perception in your world? What temporary "Band-Aid solutions" are you using to solve permanent problems? What are the things you have turned a blind eye to that need to be reexamined? The things you don't see any more because you have become so used to them?

What is the 'better way' in your world? Once that is determined, you can make positive changes occur.

## Take Action!

1. Take a moment to observe your work space and habits.

2. Ask yourself, "Is there a better way?"

3. Make minor change for major impact.

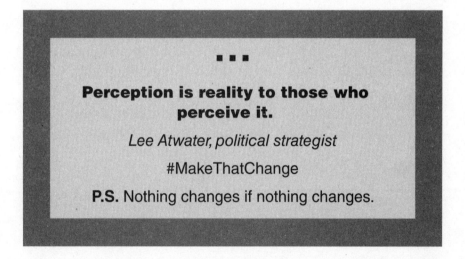

**■ ■ ■**

**Perception is reality to those who perceive it.**

*Lee Atwater, political strategist*

#MakeThatChange

**P.S.** Nothing changes if nothing changes.

# 43

# THREE MAGIC SECRETS TO A HAPPY LIFE

**Q.** Do you want to know the secret to happiness?

**A.** It's three key things:
1. Expectation Management
2. Self-Acceptance
3. Flexibility and Adaptability

According to James Taylor, "The secret of life is enjoying the passage of time." Inevitably things can and will go wrong and you will be faced with challenges that will be quite trying. This book was written with the purpose of making any difficulties you may face in business and life less gripping, less intense, and less lasting by using tangible and proven tools, techniques, and strategies to help you.

Albert Einstein once said:

"Let us not strive to be people of success.
Let us strive to be people of value."

Summary: If you are of value to your friends, family, clients, and community,
Then you truly are a success.

My wish for you is that you have found value by reading, applying, and sharing the Golden Nuggets in this book.

---

## Take Action!

1. What new expectations can you set for yourself?
2. What can you do to be happy and accepting of *you*?
3. Can you be more flexible and adaptable?

#HappyLiving

**P.S.** Don't postpone joy!

# 44

# WHAT'S YOUR "ONE THING"?

**Q.** Have you ever come to the end of a business "how-to" book and wondered how you were going to apply it all?

**A.** There is an old Italian expression: Remember, you can't boil the ocean (Ricorda, non puoi far bollire l'oceano!), but you can get a pot of water and boil that, meaning don't try to do too much too soon. Pick your most preferred Golden Nuggets and practice, practice, practice. Then, as they become habits, add more, and more and more.

Now that Part 4 of this book has come to an end, it would be a good idea to reflect on what you have read. Take a moment and flip back through the pages and note below the Golden Nuggets you would like to use before moving on to your new work life habits to maintain beyond this book.

Is it taking action on applying the Corporate Culture Code, pursuing closure on dormant goals like The White House Story (Part 2), being aware of the Persistence of Perception, or applying the Three Magic Secrets to a Happy Life? Once your list is complete, rank the top three things you will do differently, and commit to doing your "one thing" today.

**Favorite Golden Nuggets**

_____

_____

_____

_____

Top three Golden Nuggets in order of importance:

1. _____

2. _____

3. _____

The "one thing" I will commit to do first is:

_____

_____

## Take Action!

1. Ask yourself each business day, "What's the one thing I can do to further my success for tomorrow?"

2. Do it!

3. Leave your day feeling satisfied!

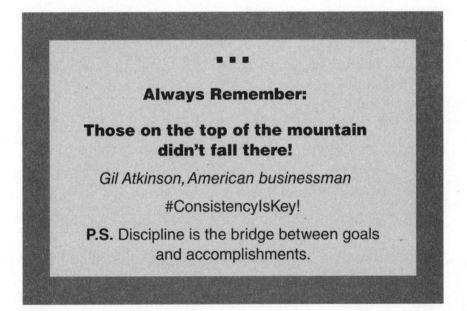

■ ■ ■

**Always Remember:**

**Those on the top of the mountain didn't fall there!**

*Gil Atkinson, American businessman*

#ConsistencyIsKey!

**P.S.** Discipline is the bridge between goals and accomplishments.

## 45

# FINAL THOUGHTS AND PARTING GIFTS

**Q.** Looking for more Golden Nuggets and Precious Joy Gems?

**A.** You already have all that you need to succeed!

So … Time for a Purple Break?

Now that you have finished this book, it's the perfect time to cover your eyes, relax, and breathe. While restoring your visual purple (Chapter 1), take a moment to reflect on what you have read. Once your Purple Break is over, refer back and review the 'One Thing' sections to create your strategy moving forward.

**Always remember:** All is well, all is well, all is perfectly well and unfolding as it will, so continue to walk with confidence in the direction of your dreams. I promise to be with you in spirit every step of the way as you continue to create more *Joy in Business (and in life)* for yourself and others.

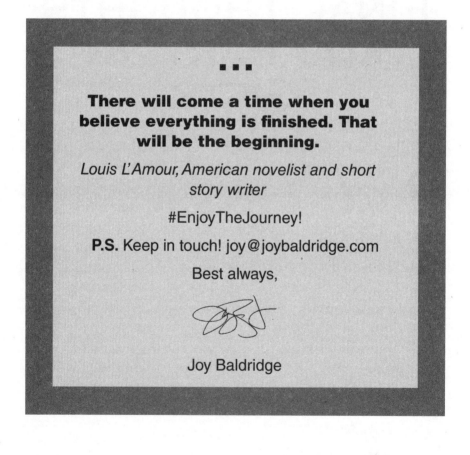

■ ■ ■

**There will come a time when you believe everything is finished. That will be the beginning.**

*Louis L'Amour, American novelist and short story writer*

#EnjoyTheJourney!

**P.S.** Keep in touch! joy@joybaldridge.com

Best always,

Joy Baldridge

# MEET JOY BALDRIDGE

*Purple Breaks are great!*

Joy Baldridge, CPS, CSP, is an engaging and sought-after keynote speaker and TEDx presenter who helps the best companies in the world become even better at increasing revenue and productivity while decreasing frustration and stress. Her areas of expertise are leadership, sales, team building, communication, and positive change management.

She is the founder and president of Baldridge Seminars International and Top Notch Training and Development. Both firms focus on providing real-world, innovative, actionable, life-changing tools that yield profitable results. Joy's first speaking engagement was at the White House at the age of 19. She got there by cold calling the president.

Joy works with the best companies in the world with the sole goal to make the best even better by increasing sales, productivity, and profitability, while decreasing frustration and stress. She speaks at national sales meetings, conventions, and association conferences both domestically and globally. She is also a writer who custom-designs and delivers engaging and entertaining sales, management, and leadership programs and retreats that get results.

For more information on Joy go to www.joybaldridge.com or call/text 203–564–0141. For more Facebook Live Streams, visit www.facebook.com/JoyBaldridgeCSP. To book Joy for powerful and uplifting keynote presentations, sales training, or retreat facilitation email: joy@joybaldridge.com

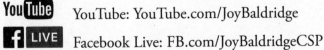

 YouTube: YouTube.com/JoyBaldridge

Facebook Live: FB.com/JoyBaldridgeCSP

Twitter: Twitter.com/in/JoyBaldridge

LinkedIn: Linkedin.com/in/JoyBaldridge

WhatsApp: JoyBaldridge

Snapchat: Joy Baldridge

# THE JOY GEM GLOSSARY

## TANGIBLE GOLDEN NUGGETS FOR CREATING A MORE POSITIVE WORK ENVIRONMENT AND EXCEPTIONAL CUSTOMER EXPERIENCE

### Always Flexible and Adaptable (AFA)

AFA is the foundation of the "Joy Experience!" According to *Fortune* magazine, you have to possess two characteristics to be employed in this millennium, flexibility and adaptability, because if you're rigid you'll break, and what good is it to be broken? The definition of flexibility is to bend without breaking. The definition of adaptability is to adjust to circumstances. AFA All the way! Always Flexible and Adaptable!

### It's OK

It's OK is best said before saying AFA. For example, when anything goes wrong, no matter how challenging or unexpected, if your response to yourself is, "It's OK, because I'm Always Flexible and Adaptable!" It defuses the tension and stress of the situation. It doesn't necessarily mean that what happened is OK. It means that *you're* OK. It helps you deal better with trying circumstances and keep your cool. (. . . Like Bob.)

### BOB

Bob is a yellow character who is the mascot of the concept of Always Flexible and Adaptable (AFA). He stretches far and always bounces back fast. And you can, too! Continuously be aware of how to be more like Bob by stretching your capabilities and bouncing back faster from adversity.

### Certified AFA

Certified AFA is the gold standard of always being flexible and adaptable. You handle change and unexpected things with ease. You adapt well to all circumstances.

## Worry, Anxiety, and Fear (WAF)

Watch your WAFs. Detect and deflect them and then say goodbye to them by saying, "Goodbye worry, goodbye anxiety, so long fear, and hello joy!" This works because 90% of what you worry about doesn't even happen. Feel free to test this theory. Worry does little to change a situation. It's a waste of time and energy. Anxiety is the horrible stories we tell ourselves that are rarely if ever true. Fear is counterproductive. Choosing faith over fear works. You just have to believe. Zig Ziglar said fear as an acronym can mean one of two things: Fear Everything And Run! or Face Everything And Rise! HINT: Pick number 2!

## Acknowledge and Release

When you acknowledge what is bothering you, you have the power to release it sooner versus later. What you ignore tends to grow and become all-consuming. Face your concerns head on. Say to them: "I see you and you are not welcome here." When you acknowledge anything that is upsetting or of concern, it automatically is released.

## Over It!

When you have a stressful or troubling thought that lingers, self-commands can work well. Two self-commands have been proven to work effectively. "Over it!" Is one. Sometimes you have to just build a bridge and get over it! "Enough!" is another (see the next Joy Gem).

## Enough!

Enough is the perfect word to say to yourself when you find yourself obsessing over something you wish or didn't happen the way you wanted. By saying "Enough!" several times, you help ease your mind. Give it a try: "Enough!"

## Be Kind

Being kind to yourself is essential for your mental and physical well-being. I don't know why we are so hard on ourselves, but we are, and it does us no good. Instead, be kind to yourself. Say nice things. Catch yourself doing something right!

## All Is Well

One nice thing you can say to yourself is, "All is well, all is well, all is perfectly well, and unfolding as it should." If you repeat this mantra from Robert Adams over and over and over (a technique called "flooding" by Émile Coué, the French inventor), it will help you to achieve peace of mind, even on the most stressful days.

**Cut the Worry Wires**

Worry does nothing productive. You can cut the worry wires any time you wish by acknowledging what your worries are and then doing whatever it takes to prevent them from coming up again. Use your hands to imitate scissors and actually cut the worry wires.

**Function in Disaster, Finish in Style!**

The key is to keep going and not let any circumstances stop you. It's easy to shut down or freeze up when faced with difficult situations. If you keep going despite any adversity, you will have a much better outcome.

**4–4–6**

The 4–4–6 breathing exercise puts you in the present tense. It helps you stay calm and focused on your priorities. To do the 4–4–6 inhale for 4 seconds. Try it now: 1, 2, 3, 4. Hold it for 4 seconds: 1, 2, 3, 4. And exhale for 6 seconds: 1, 2,

3, 4, 5, 6. Repeat often. Deep breathing is your most easily accessible, yet most underutilized, stress reducer. You can access it at any time. The best time to do the 4–4–6 is now. And since there is no time other than now, do it often and see what happens.

**Now Is Perfect**

Now is perfect. Test it at any time. It's rare that we fully experience the now because our thoughts tend to race to a future or past concern. Deep breathing puts you in the now. The 4–4–6 (the Joy Gem above) is an instant way to become more present and gain clarity of thought and achieve focused, productive execution. Take a breath, take a moment, and ask yourself: "What is the best use of my time *right now*?" Then do the thing that comes to mind. Yes, now is perfect. And the only time you ever truly have is now.

**T Press**

T Press stands for Toe Press. When you find yourself in a stressful or intimidating situation, try pressing your toes firmly into the ground. It will keep you calm and "grounded." The more intense the encounter, the harder you press down on your toes. The T Press allows you to appear calm and relaxed in your facial expressions, voice tone, and body language while all the tension goes to your toes, where no one can see it. Give it a try and see how it can work for you! The T Press works especially well when giving presentations.

## With Ease

Language is behavior and behavior is language. Words are containers of power. Saying "with ease" after anything you experience today can only make it better. For instance: "I'm dealing with this difficult situation. . .with ease." "I am stuck in traffic. . . with ease." "I'm stressed out. . . with ease." The absurdity of it may even make you laugh. Doing everything "with ease" makes for a better day.

## Salt the Hay

"Salt the Hay" is a Baldridge family motto that originated from the well-known expression: "You can bring a horse to water, but you can't make him drink." Horses are stubborn. They won't always drink. What can you do? You can salt the hay. What happens when you salt the hay? The horse will get thirsty and drink! So when faced with a situation that seems to be at a dead end, remember to "Salt the Hay" and find a way!

## Find a Way!

When you adopt the Salt the Hay mindset (most recent Joy Gem), finding a way when it seems like there is no way is how you must start to think. By looking at a situation in different ways and asking yourself, "How can we salt the hay on this?" you will become a better problem-solver and solution-seeker. After all, there are no problems in life—only situations with an abundance of possible solutions.

## Can't Can't Can

Behind every two can'ts there is a can. When we try something and it doesn't work, we try again, and when that doesn't work, it's easy to say, well, I tried, and I tried again. Instead, say this: "I can't do this, and I can't do that, so what *can* I do?" And watch more answers appear.

## How's Your Ogive?

The Ogive curve is a cumulative frequency curve in statistics. There is Positive Ogive and Negative Ogive. Positive Ogive is when the points on the curve ascend and Negative Ogive is when the points on the curve descend. The analogy is that life is like an Ogive curve. Both positive points and negative points can be plotted on the graph. The question to ask yourself is: "How's my Ogive?" At any moment you can check in with yourself and see how your day is going. If on a scale of 1 to 10 your Ogive is positive (an 8 or 9), that's great! Keep going, you are on a roll. But if you find negativity is starting to consume you, you are experiencing Negative Ogive and you have to do something to pull yourself out of it. Negative Ogive is like quicksand. It can pull you down if you let it. What's best is to detect and deflect it. When you ask, "How's my Ogive?" and find that it is low on a 1 to 10 scale, you can acknowledge that you are experiencing some Negative Ogive and work toward pulling out of it. Acknowledging when things aren't going as you wish helps you release the negativity and start moving in a better direction. (See Acknowledge and Release above.)

## No Negative Ogive

By adopting the mindset of No Negative Ogive you set a standard for your thoughts. It's easy to get in a bad mood and be upset about things that happen in your day, but if you detect that Negative Ogive is happening, you Can take action to bring yourself up and out of it. Some examples of how to escape from Negative Ogive are as follows: Say positive things to yourself such as, "All is well" (Joy Gem above), listen to music, do something you are good at and that you enjoy, take a brief break and regroup.

## Stay Above the Line

A line separates Positive and Negative Ogive on the graph (see Figure G.1). Your goal is to detect and deflect negative Ogive so you can stay above the line.

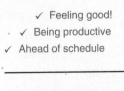

✓ Feeling good!
✓ Being productive
✓ Ahead of schedule

+ **Positive Ogive**

———————————————— *Stay Above the Line*

✗ Behind schedule
✗ Too many interruptions
✗ Feeling awful!

– **Negative Ogive**

**Figure G.1   Stay in the positive on the Ogive graph.**

## House of Glad

The House of Glad is a term I created to stay happy more often. It's a place that is accessible to everyone to live a positive and productive life. If you watch your Ogive (see above Joy Gem) and keep working toward adding more Positive Ogive into your world while working at detecting and deflecting any Negative Ogive, you will create a happier and better way of living.

## Mad, Glad, Sad, Scared

The four core human emotions are Mad, Glad, Sad, and Scared. I call them houses. So you have the House of Mad, the House of Glad, the House of Sad, and the House of Scared. Ask yourself which house you live in most. Is it time to move? You have the capacity to move! Knowing you have the capacity to move and deciding to move to the House of Glad can change things for the better. Of course, being human, you will experience all the houses each day as things happen. Making the House of Glad your primary residence gives you a positive place to go back to once things settle down. It is important to remember that *you can choose*

which house you want to be your primary residence. It takes just as much work to live in the House of Glad as it does to live in the house of Mad, Sad, or Scared; things will go wrong and you will have to deal with them, but going home to the House of Glad is the best.

## R.E.N.T.

To live in the House of Glad (see Joy Gems above), you have to "Pay your R.E.N.T. every day." R.E.N.T. stands for Rest, Exercise, Nutrition, and Thoughts. By paying attention to rest, exercise, nutrition, and your thoughts during your day, you will have more positive and productive days.

## Purple Break

Ken Baldridge (my father) invented the Purple Break in 1967 when he learned about rhodopsin (also known as visual purple). This pigment breaks down in bright light, causing fatigue, and is restored in total darkness. A Purple Break is when you cover your eyes, relax, and breathe to restore the visual purple, which leads to energy renewal. Try it now. Cover your eyes. Make sure it is totally dark. Now count backwards from 20 to 1 on each exhaled breath.

That's 20, exhale, relax; 19, exhale, relax; and so on. Find a discrete and safe place to take your Purple Break(s) and feel the stress and pressures of the day dissolve.

## The Platinum Rule

The Platinum Rule is to treat people the way *they* want to be treated, as opposed to the Golden Rule, which is treating people the way *you* want to be treated. It is helpful when applying the Platinum Rule to understand the four personality types you will deal with.

## Social, Factual, Helpful, Driven

Each personality type speaks a language, the Language of the Land. Those from the Land of Social frequently use words like great, amazing, and rock star. Those from the Land of Factual frequently use words such as you're right, absolutely right, and perfection. Those from the Land of Helpful frequently use words like you're helpful, very helpful, and love it! Those from the Land of Driven do not speak very much or use many words when communicating. They'd rather do something instead of talking about it. But the words that pertain to them are win, you win, and number 1. If you hear any of these words, it will help you detect where the person's land of origin is and give you the opportunity to relate better to him or her by repeating the words that they most frequently use.

In essence, you will be speaking their language. Words are containers of power and the way you speak specific words can help you to make more positive connections with people and foster stronger and more meaningful relationships.

Social Speak: Language of the Land

Great!

You're AMAZING!

Hot Potato

Rock Star!

Factual Speak: Language of the Land

Right

You're Right

Absolutely RIGHT

Perfection!

Helpful Speak: Language of the Land

Helpful

You're Helpful

Very Helpful

Love it!

Driven Speak: Language of the Land

Win

You WIN

Number 1

## Chameleon

Chameleon is a personality type that is hard to detect because it is so close to the border of all the types. With the chameleon you can use any of the words of the lands and see which ones resonate.

## Joy!

Joy is a source or cause of great happiness! It is something or someone that delights. It is to be happy in the success of yourself or others. Spreading joy throughout your day leads to the best outcomes. Joy is contagious. Create a 'Joy Experience' for everyone you encounter. Look for ways to make someone's day and you surely will!

## Really?

"Really?" is a conversation extender. When you say, "Really?" in a nice voice tone it expresses interest and shows engagement. It can be followed by a question such as, "Why is that?" Or used alone. It is a sign of a very good listener.

## Bite Your Tongue (BYT)

Practice gently biting your tongue to improve your listening skills. Good listeners are quite rare. It is easy to impulsively speak when interacting with others. Better is to ask questions and listen before speaking. Since you can't listen and talk at the same time, gently biting your tongue will prevent you from talking and help you to listen. It takes discipline, but it's worth it. The best way to break an old habit is to replace it with a new habit. The old habit was to interrupt, the new habit can be to gently bite your tongue, actively listen, and wait for your turn to speak. You can discretely say "Bite your tongue" to yourself or a co-worker as code to stop talking.

## Take a Sip

To be a better listener it is important to speak less and listen more. If it is appropriate to have a beverage you can sip when interacting, you can choreograph your sips with the questions you ask to prevent you from speaking too much or making assumptions that you blurt out. When you have the impulse to interrupt or speak, try asking a question instead such as, "What can I do to help?" or "What do you need to know first?" And then take a sip, let the person speak, and listen closely.

## Velvet Hammer

Since words are containers of power, the Velvet Hammer is a way to speak candidly and directly with kindness and sensitivity. Velvet Hammer words are carefully selected and are smooth and soft like velvet, but pack a punch (like a hammer) and get results! A few of the most popular Velvet Hammer words are, "noticed" and "wondering," as in "I *noticed* that you have been coming to work later than usual, and I was *wondering* how to prevent that in the future."

## No "Should"

Should can be very destructive. Listen for the "should" words in your mind or when you speak. It is counterproductive and can cause frustration and upset to use them. It may sound like this, "They *should* know better!" "I *should* get onto that project." "I *should* lose weight/work out." Should can be self-defeating. Whenever you feel the word should coming to mind, you need to have an expectation conversation with yourself or others wherein you say what is happening and agree on what needs to be done about it. A good way to replace the should habit is to "Just do it!"

## Before, During, and After (BDA)

Be aware of how you interact with team members or customers before, during, and after you speak with them. *Before:* How are you greeting them? *During:* Are you actively listening and asking questions to understand how to best serve them? *After* your conversation, what is the last thing they experienced as they left you? Remember, your goodbyes are as important as your hellos, both on the phone and in person. In psychological theory, the Primacy Effect is your first impression and the Recency Effect is your most recent encounter or last impression. Paying attention during the conversation brings greater trust and likability. So watch your BDA every day!

## Plus, Plus, Dash (PPD)

PPD means being prepared to say two positive things (plus, plus) and then politely dashing off. By applying the PPD you have the ability to minimize conversations, politely get to the point and take action, so you can save yourself and others time and leave people with a positive feeling. An example of the PPD is: "Thank you for calling, I'm happy to help with this, I'll get right on it." Done! If everyone on your team knows the PPD code, you can just say, "PPD 3?" Which means, "Happy to help, can we chat at 3:00?" *Caution:* You cannot always apply the PPD. Watch for ways you can, because when you do it regularly, it will save you 3 to 5 hours a week. PPD!

## No "But"

*But* acts as a verbal eraser. It erases anything that comes before it. So if you use the PPD and say, "but," it ruins the effect. For example: "I'm glad you called and I want to help, but I'm so busy." is not as effective as "I'm glad you called and I want to help. Right now I'm under a tight deadline. When can we reconnect?" It is OK to use the word *but* if you want to minimize what comes before it. For instance: "I know it's been a long time, but it will be ready today!" A good use of but is when good news follows it.

## What's Your Mission?

Asking yourself each day "What's my mission for the day?" creates a self-motivation mindset, because most people strive to reach their missions. If you are an overachiever, you may want to ask yourself, "What's my mission for the morning?" and "What's my mission for the afternoon?" Give it a try and see how much more you can and will accomplish. These mission questions provide clarity of thought and focused execution. You will feel more energized when on a mission each and every day.

## What's Your "One Thing"?

"What's the one thing you can do to further your success for tomorrow?" A successful CEO asks himself that at the end of each day to build momentum by doing the activities that have the most importance and impact. He said asking this question enabled him to get more important things done and leave each day feeling satisfied. Can you ask yourself this question at the end of each day? Watch what happens. It can be quite magical!

## It Will Never Be Yesterday

It is so true that it will never be yesterday. So what are you going to do today to further your success for tomorrow? Use the Joy Gems and watch your success soar!!

# APPENDIX

## RHODOPSIN*

Rhodopsin, also known as visual purple, is a biological pigment in photoreceptor cells of the retina that is responsible for the first events in the perception of light, enabling vision in low-light conditions. Exposed to light, the pigment immediately photobleaches, and it takes about 45 minutes to regenerate fully in humans. Its discovery was reported by German physiologist Franz Christian Boll in 1876.

Rhodopsin consists of the protein moietyopsin and a reversibly covalently boundcofactor, retinal. Opsin, a bundle of seven transmembrane helices connected to each other by protein loops, binds retinal (a photoreactive chromophore), which is located in a central pocket on the seventh helix at a lysine residue. Retinal lies horizontally with relation to the membrane. Each outer segment disc contains thousands of visual pigment molecules. About half the opsin is within the lipid bilayer. Retinol is produced in theretina from Vitamin A, from dietary beta-carotene.

Rhodopsin of the rods most strongly absorbs green-blue light and, therefore, appears reddish-purple, which is why it is also called "visual purple." It is responsible for *monochromatic* vision in the dark.

Humans have four different other opsins besides rhodopsin. The photopsins are found in the different types of the cone cells of the retina and are the basis of color vision. They have absorption maxima for yellowish-green (photopsin I), green (photopsin II), and bluish-violet (photopsin III) light. The remaining opsin (melanopsin) is found in photosensitive ganglion cells and absorbs blue light most strongly.

The structure of rhodopsin has been studied in detail via x-ray crystallography on rhodopsin crystals.

---

* Wikipedia

## FATIGUE COSTS BUSINESS BILLIONS IN LOST PRODUCTIVITY

During lunchtime conversation with her work colleagues, Melanie appeared distracted and distant. She tried to feign her interest with the occasional nod of her head. Her head was clouded with fog when she realized that the conversation around her had stopped.

"So what do you think, Mel?" Summoning all her powers of concentration, Mel suddenly jolted with fright at the realization of her three friends looking at her intently.

"Are you alright?" they asked.

"I'm sorry guys. I'm just exhausted. I had a terrible night's sleep and it's been a struggle to keep my eyes open all day."

It's an all-too-familiar scenario in the workplaces and homes today. With the increasing trend in Western life to cram more and more into each day, we are craving for more energy and more balance in our lives while, at the same time, also maintaining our productivity. However, the major epidemic is that the majority of us simply do not have the time or the energy to do the things that we really want to do.

Today's time-strapped lifestyle has turned most of our lives into a day-to-day struggle for survival before we crawl into bed exhausted at the end of the day. Fatigue is not just creating strains at home, but the workplace is definitely feeling the pinch.

According to a recent study by the American College of Occupational and Environmental Medicine (ACOEM),* fatigue is costing the workplace in the United States $136 billion in health-related lost productivity. Thirty-nine percent of the 29,000 U.S. workers interviewed said that they had experienced "low levels of energy, poor sleep, or a feeling of fatigue."

The biggest cause of productivity losses from fatigue was not from having days absent but $114 billion were lost in productivity due to reduced performance while at work. This mainly came from poor concentration, requiring more time to complete normal tasks.

Along with the common cold and body aches and pains, a lack of energy is one of the most common health complaints in Western society, yet it is a condition that very few of us seek professional help for because a lack of energy, by itself, is not fatal. We fail to understand that the lifestyle factors that cause the vast majority of cases of fatigue, if continued, can go on and contribute to the development of the most common life-threatening conditions such as heart disease, obesity, and diabetes.

Fatigue is one of the health signs that you should all take immediate notice of. It is the first indicator that your body is starting to struggle to work properly. Recurrent fatigue occurs when your body is spending more and more energy on trying to repair the damage you inflict on yourself, so less energy is available for you to use.

Unfortunately, when we do try to address our lack of energy by ourselves, we tend not to address the direct causes of the fatigue, such as managing emotional stress, trying to fit too much in, lack of exercise, lack of rest, and various other aspects of the modern, on-the-go lifestyle. Instead we opt for the over-consumption and abuse and reliance on certain foods and drinks that give us a short-term energy boost.

* J Occup Environ Med. 2007 Jan; 49(1):1-10 https://doi.org/10.1097/01. jom.0000249782.60321.2a

# INDEX

Page references followed by *fig* indicate an illustrated figure or photograph.